12

W9-CBH-771

From: ~~Jean~~
Annie
I love you so
much! (Almost
as much as
Jesus!)

He loves Me!

_10AM_

The Relationship God Has

Always Wanted With You

2/10 toe curls
10 lifts
3-5 stretches
3-5 towel

Wayne Jacobsen

HE LOVES ME! by Wayne Jacobsen

Published by:
Insight Publishing Group
8801 South Yale, Suite 410
Tulsa, OK 74137
918-493-1718

Except where otherwise indicated, all Scripture quotations are from the Holy Bible, New International Version. Copyright © 1973, 1978, 1984 by the International Bible Society. Used by permission of Zondervan Bible Publishers.

International Standard Book Number: 1-930027-04-4

Library of Congress Card Catalog Number: 00-103886

1 2 3 4 5 6 7 8 CHG 04 03 02 01 00

Printed in the United States of America

To Sara,

On the celebration of our 25th wedding anniversary

I couldn't have found a better friend or beloved partner with whom I could share this journey. Your example of loving me through my worst moments and laying down your life at great personal sacrifice has taught me more about God's love and how I can trust him freely than anyone else on the planet.

Acknowledgments

Thank you, Kevin Smith, David Boan, and John Yates of Australia, for pulling me aside and showing me a more excellent way. Your insights on the cross revolutionized my appreciation for Father's love and helped me understand how Jesus' church can really share his life together.

Thank you, Dave and Donna Coleman of Visalia, for enriching my life and this book with the lessons you've learned and being patient with us as we went through a similar process.

Thank you, Nick Sembrano and Bob Blasingame for contributing your expertise to the specific content of these pages.

Thank you, Scott and Sandi Tompkins for adding your special gifts of editing to this manuscript.

Thank you, John Mason and your staff at Insight International for helping me make this book available to those who will be touched by it.

Thank you, dear friends in and around my former home town of Visalia, California, for all the ways you have loved me, stood by me and shared my journey. And thank you, too, to the many explorers we have met from all over the world who are on a similar journey to discover the depths of God's love and how to live as his people in the earth.

Contents

Foreword 6

THE RELATIONSHIP GOD HAS ALWAYS WANTED WITH YOU

1. Daisy Petal Christianity 9
2. What Jesus' Disciples Didn't Know 17
3. Threatened With Hell. 25
4. A Father Like No Other. 33
5. Welcome Home. 41

WHAT FEAR CAN NEVER ACHIEVE

6. The Tyranny of the Favor Line 49
7. What Shall I Give to God? 59
8. The Businessman and the Beggar 67
9. The God We Love to Fear 75
10. The Most Powerful Force in the Universe 83

UNDENIABLE PROOF

11. He Loved You Enough to Let You Go 93
12. Who Needed the Sacrifice? 101
13. The Hen and Her Chicks. 107
14. What Really Happened on the Cross. 115
15. The Antidote for Sin 123
16. In the Darkest Moment . . . Trust. 131

A LIFE LIVED IN LOVE

17. Trying to Earn Points With Someone
    Who Is No Longer Keeping Score 139
18. So Sin Isn't Important to God? 147
19. A Lifetime of Learning to Trust 153
20. Shamelessly Free 161
21. In Exactly the Same Way 169
22. The Prayer God Always Answers. 177
Discussion Questions 185

Foreword

With wise words and thorough logic, Wayne Jacobsen leaves no obstacle standing between a believer and God the Father. He carefully and gently pushes aside any resistance to absolute reliance on the grace of God and his plan for us. Some journeys carry such dangers and mysteries that we long for a hand to hold and a secure face to be seen. This book places your hand in the secure one and clearly portrays the face of God.

When Jesus answered a questioner and informed us that the greatest commandment was to "love God with all our heart, soul, mind and strength," for many of us, this was a command to which we could only aspire. Perhaps we even prayed, "Lord, I want to love you with all my heart, soul, mind and strength." After reading this book, I am confident you will easily say, "I do love you completely."

No matter what your emotional state, peace will settle on your heart. Any anxieties about God are going to fade. Prepare your face for a smile and your heart for a constant parade of brass bands celebrating a great victory.

As you read and receive the understandings of this book, you will frequent God's presence much more because of the eternal relationship you will find there so superior to your own best efforts or dreams. These gifts of God are unattainable on your own but you will find this book to be an invitation to God's house and its warmth with an RSVP. With that invitation in hand, you will feel like you have "arrived;" and you have!

If it seems that I push too hard and compliment too highly about this book, it is on purpose. You hold in your hands a classic.

Be prepared to know God better and love him more. You are about to go on a journey whose road map you will save for repeat use and whose copies you will gladly and freely give to others.

—GAYLE D. ERWIN
AUTHOR, *Jesus Style*

The Relationship God Has Always Wanted With You

On that day you will realize

that I am in my Father,

and you are in me,

and I am in you.

—John 14:20

Daisy Petal Christianity

He loves me.
He loves me not.
He loves me.
He loves me not.

The little girl stands in the backyard chanting as she plucks petals one by one from the daisy and drops them to the ground. At game's end, the last petal tells all; whether or not the person desired returns the affection.

Of course no one takes it seriously, and if children don't get the answer they desire they take another daisy and start again. It doesn't take long even for children to realize that flowers weren't designed to tell romantic fortunes. Why should they link their hearts' desires to the fickleness of chance?

Why indeed! But it is a lesson far easier learned in romance than in more spiritual pursuits. For long after we've put away our daisies, many of us continue to play the game with God.

HE LOVES ME!

This time we don't pluck flower petals, but probe through our circumstances trying to figure out exactly how God feels about us.

I got a raise. *He loves me.*

I didn't get the promotion I wanted, or I lost my job altogether. *He loves me not!*

Something in the Bible inspired me today. *He loves me!*

My child is seriously ill. *He loves me not!*

I gave money to someone in need. *He loves me!*

I let my anger get the best of me. *He loves me not!*

Something for which I prayed actually happened. *He loves me!*

I stretched the truth to get myself out of a tight spot. *He loves me not!*

A friend calls me unexpectedly to encourage me. *He loves me!*

My car needs a new transmission. *He loves me not!*

A PERILOUS TIGHTROPE

I have played that game most of my life, trying to sort out in any given moment how God might feel about me personally. I grew up learning that he is a God of love, and for the most part I believed it to be true.

In good times, nothing is easier to believe. In days when my family was healthy and our relationships a joy; when my ministry thrived and both income and opportunity were increasing; when we had plenty of time to enjoy our friends and were not burdened down with need; who wouldn't be certain of God's love?

But that certainty eroded when those times of bliss were interrupted with more troublesome events...

...like a childhood condition that provided no end of embarrassment.

...or the day one of my friends in high school died of a brain tumor even as we prayed earnestly for his healing.

...or when I wasn't selected for a job I wanted in college because someone had lied about me.

...or the night my house was robbed.

...or when I was severely burned in a kitchen accident.

...or when I watched my father-in-law and my brother, both die with debilitating illnesses even though they sought God earnestly for healing.

...or when colleagues in ministry lied to me and spread false stories about me to win the support of others.

...or when I didn't know from where my next paycheck would come.

...or when I saw my wife crushed by circumstances that I couldn't get God to change no matter how hard I tried.

...or when doors of opportunity that appeared certain to open would suddenly slam shut like a wind-blown door.

Then I wondered how God really felt about me. I couldn't understand how a God who loved me would either allow such things into my life or wouldn't fix them immediately so that I or people I loved wouldn't have to endure such pain.

He loves me not! Or so I thought on those days. My disappointment at God could easily turn two directions. Often in my pain and frustration, when I felt like I had done enough to deserve better, I would rail at God like the Job of old, accusing him of either being unfair or unloving. In more honest moments, however, I was well aware of the temptations and failures that could exclude me from his care. I would come out of those times committed to trying harder to live the life I thought would merit his love.

I lived for 34 years as a believer on this perilous tightrope. Even when there was no crisis hanging over my head, I was always wary of the next one God might drop on me at any second if I couldn't stay on his good side. In some ways I had become like the schizophrenic child of an abusive father, never certain what God I'd meet on any given day—the one who wanted to scoop me up in his arms with laughter, or the one who would ignore me or punish me for reasons I could never understand.

Only in the last five years have I discovered that my methods of discerning God's love were as flawed as pulling petals from a daisy. I haven't been the same since.

CONVINCING EVIDENCE

What about you?

Have you ever felt tossed back and forth by circumstances occasionally certain, but mostly uncertain about how the Creator of the universe feels about you? Or perhaps you've never even known how much God loves you.

In a Bible study recently, I met a forty-year-old woman who was active in her fellowship but admitted to a small group of us that she had never been certain that God loved her. She seemed to want to tell me more, but finally only asked me to pray for her.

As I did, asking God to reveal just how much he loved her, an image came to mind. I saw a figure I knew to be Jesus walking through a meadow hand in hand with a little girl about five years old. Somehow I knew this woman was that little girl. I prayed that he would help her discover a childlikeness of spirit that would allow her to skip through the meadows with him.

When I finished praying I looked up at her eyes that were brimming with tears.

"Did you say 'meadow'?" she asked.

I nodded, thinking it odd she had focused on that word.

Immediately she began to cry. As she was able to speak, she said, "I wasn't sure I wanted to tell you. When I was five years old I was molested in a meadow by an older boy. Whenever I think about God, I think about that horrible event and I wonder why, if he loved me so much, he didn't stop that from happening."

She's not alone. Many people carry scars and disappointments that can appear to be convincing evidence that the God of love might not exist, or if he does, maintains a safe distance from them and leaves them to the whim of other people's sins.

I don't have a stock answer for moments like that, as if any could be effective in the midst of such pain. I told her, that evidently God wanted her to know he had been there with her, and although he didn't act in the only way she could understand true love to act, that he loved her nonetheless. He wanted to walk her through that defiled meadow and redeem it in her life.

He wanted to give her a measure of joy in the face of the most traumatic event of her life and turn what was supposed to destroy her into a stepping stone toward grace. I know that can sound almost trite in the face of such incredible pain, but the process has begun for her. It is my hope these words will encourage that process in you, as well.

PERCEPTION VERSUS REALITY

For truly God has never acted towards us in any way other than with a depth of love that defies human understanding. I know it may not look like that at times. When he seems to callously disregard our most noble prayers, our trust in him can be easily shattered and we wonder if he cares for us. We can even come up with a list of our own failures that can seemingly justify God's indifference and beckon us into a dark whirlpool of self-loathing.

When we're playing the he-loves-me-he-loves-me-not-game, the evidence against God can appear overwhelming. For reasons we shall see throughout these pages, God does not often do the things we think his love would compel him to do for us. He often seems to stand by with indifference while we suffer. How often does he seem to disappoint our most noble expectations?

But perception is not necessarily reality. If we define God

only in our limited interpretation of our own circumstances, we will never discover who he really is.

However, he has provided a far better way, where our daisy-petal approach to Christianity can be swallowed up by the undeniable proof of his love for us on the cross of Calvary. That's the side of the cross that has all but been ignored in recent decades. We have not seen what really happened there between the Father and his Son that opens the door to his love so vast and so certain that it cannot be challenged even by your darkest days.

Through that door we can really know who God is and embrace the relationship with him that the deepest part of our heart has hungered to experience. That is where we'll begin, because it is only in the context of the relationship God desires with us that we can begin to discover the full glory of his love.

He does love you more deeply than you've ever imagined; and he has done so throughout your entire life. Once you embrace that truth, your troubles will never again drive you to question God's affection for you or whether you've done enough to merit it. Instead of fearing he has turned his back on you, you will be able to trust his love at the moments you need him most. You will even see in the strangest ways how that love can flow out of you to touch a world starved for it.

Learning to trust him like that is not something any of us can resolve in an instant; but something we'll grow to discover for the whole of our lives. God knows how difficult it is for us to accept his love and teaches us with more patience than we've ever known. Through every circumstance and in the most surprising ways, he makes his love known to us in ways we can understand.

So perhaps it's time to toss your daisies aside and discover that it is not the fear of losing God's love that will keep you on his path, but the simple joy of living in it every day.

On the day you discover that, you will truly begin to live!

How great is the love the Father has lavished on us, that we should be called children of God! And that is what we are!
—1 John 3:1

For your personal journey

How often do you find yourself doubting God's love for you? When do you find you question His love the most? How certain are you that God loves you as deeply as he does anyone else in the world? When difficulties arise do you find yourself doubting God's love for you, or trying to be more righteous so he'll like you more? Ask God in the days ahead to reveal to you the depths of his love for you.

What Jesus' Disciples Didn't Know

God is not mute: the Word spoke, not out of a whirlwind,
but out of the human larynx of a Palestinian Jew.
PHILIP YANCEY, *THE JESUS I NEVER KNEW*

Can you imagine what it must have been like for Jesus the first moment he sat around with the circle of his disciples after they had finally become friends?

We all know what it is to get acquainted with new people, the awkward pauses and measured words as people get to know each other. Certainly the disciples went through that with Jesus. Just who was this Teacher and Miracle-worker and who were these other men who decided to follow him?

It might have happened during a conversation after a meal, or walking together on a road, but at some point they found themselves safe enough with him and each other to let their guard down. No longer measuring words or trying to impress each other, they slipped into the fruits of their burgeoning friendship—the freedom to be honest, to laugh, to ask the seemingly stupid question, and to relax in each other's presence.

What must that have felt like to Jesus? Had this been what he had always wanted?

For the first time since that cruel day in Eden, God was sitting down with people he loved and they were not cowering in fear.

For centuries since men and women had stood at great distance from God, shamed by their sin and intimidated by his holiness. With only a few notable exceptions, people wanted nothing to do with the immediacy of God's presence. When Mt. Sinai shook with thunder and earthquakes, the people begged Moses to go to God for them. God was a terrifying figure and feeling safe with him was unthinkable.

But God had never thought so. His plan to restore the fellowship with humanity that Adam and Eve had lost in their fall was unfolding. In Jesus, he was able to sit down in the company of those he loved and they were comfortable enough to engage him in a real conversation. What an incredible moment that must have been for Jesus, to be with people who were not so awed by him, that they could not enjoy his presence.

Of course, it only happened because they had no idea that it was God who stoked the fire as they sat around and laughed. For although we now know that Jesus was God incarnate on earth, they had no idea and that made all the difference.

GOD IN DISGUISE

I like arriving early at places I'm supposed to speak so that I can meet the people who've invited me and still have time to mingle among the gathering crowd. I introduce myself only by my first name and never let on that I'm the speaker. Surprisingly few people ever figure it out and so I get to engage in real conversations with the people before I speak.

I've learned that people treat me differently before they learn I'm the speaker or the author from out of town. They are so much more themselves, and willing to talk freely about their lives and their aspirations. Once they find out who I am, all of that changes. They are far more self-conscious and inhibited, preferring to focus questions on me and my work. Finding out who I am destroys the level of fellowship I enjoy most with people.

Admittedly it might be a bit misleading. I've watched people near me cringe with embarrassment when I'm finally introduced. Some even come up after and apologize for not realizing who I was and for "going on" about their children or their work, as if those things have just become trivial because of who I am. But I remind them that I was the one who asked and wouldn't have done so if I wasn't interested.

Once people put me in the guest-speaker box, it is hard for me to climb out. It usually takes a long time for people to relax and let me be the brother in Christ I really am. As confining as the guest speaker role can be for me, I suspect the God-box into which people put God is vastly worse for him. So I understand why he had to take on a disguise to have the relationship with people he had always desired.

The disciples were with the physical presence of God, and were completely unaware of it. They knew he was a man of God, of course. Who could watch his miracles and listen to his wisdom without knowing that?

On at least one occasion they identified him as the Messiah, but there was nothing in the first-century Jewish hope of the Messiah that said he would be God incarnate. They expected him to be a man, empowered by God as was Moses, David or Elijah. But the idea that God would take on human flesh and live that way on the earth would have been unthinkable.

How could the holy God live among sinful people and engage them face-to-face? Their history told of such moments when God's presence came to his people. Even the most righteous had fallen on their faces in fear and some of the most evil had died. They thought that's what God wanted, but as we'll see their response had far more to do with how sin reacted to God than how God wanted to be known.

THE UNVEILING

So God disguised himself, first as a baby in a manger, then as a young boy growing up in Nazareth and finally as a young man walking the hills of Galilee. No one had any idea God had come to live among them; and because of that no one cowered in fear or acted awkwardly with him.

For the first time since he walked the garden with Adam and Eve, God was among people the way he had always wanted to be. Broken lives were drawn to him, not repelled. His followers were secure enough in his presence to be genuine, even when that revealed their lust for power or their arrogance over others. Now God could experience the relationship he'd always wanted with his people.

Not even in the last day of his life before he was crucified had the disciples figured out who Jesus really was. Jesus said as much during the last meal he ate with them. "If you really knew me, you would know my Father as well." When the disciples questioned him on it, certain they had no idea who his Father was, he got even clearer: "Don't you know me even after I have been among you such a long time? Anyone who has seen me has seen the Father. How can you say, 'Show us the Father'?" (John 14:7-9).

But now he wanted them to know. The disguise was about to come off. "Don't you believe that I am in the Father, and that the Father is in me?" In a few hours he would be taken from them, tried, tortured and executed. The next time the disciples would see him he would be the resurrected Christ. There would be no hiding who he really was.

How would the disciples treat him then? Would they resort to cowering away in terror of his majesty? Jesus didn't want that realization to destroy the relationship he'd cultivated with them, but to make it grow even stronger.

His words in the upper room were designed to help them move the relationship they had experienced with Jesus in the flesh to the Father they didn't yet know, to the post-resurrected Christ, and to the Holy Spirit. Instead of being with them in the flesh, however, God would come and dwell within. But not only could the relationship continue there, Jesus told them it would be even better than they had already experienced with him.

> *"On that day you will realize that I am in my Father, and you are in me, and I am in you."*
>
> —JOHN 14:20

Read those words again. Having just told them that he and the Father were one because the Father was in him, now he invites them into that same relationship. You will be in me and I will be in you.

In these simple words Jesus reveals what God's desire had been from the first day of creation—to invite men and women into the relationship that God has known with himself for all eternity. It is as if they could no longer keep to themselves the joy, love, glory and trust that they had always shared together. Their purpose in creating the world was to invite us as mere creation to share the wonder of that relationship.

TENDER IMAGES

The friendship Jesus shared with his disciples was the model for the relationship he extends to you. He wants to be the voice that steers you through every situation, the peace that sets your heart at rest in trouble and the power that holds you up in the storm. He wants to be closer than your dearest friend and more faithful than any other person you've ever known.

I know it sounds preposterous. How can mere humans enjoy such a friendship with the Almighty God who created with a word all that we see? Do I dare think that he would know and care about the details of my life? Isn't it presumptuous to even imagine that this God would take delight in me, even though I still struggle with the failures of my flesh?

It would be if this were not his idea. He's the one that offered to be your loving Father—sharing life with you in ways no earthly father ever could.

Don't relegate this invitation to an abstract spiritual plane. When Scripture talks about the relationship God wants with us he borrows the most tender images of our world. He calls us young children beloved by a gracious Father; the bride of an expectant bridegroom; friends dear enough to die for and little chicks rushing under the protective wings of a hen.

He is obviously serious about the intimacy and security of a relationship with him built on love and trust. Many shy away from such thoughts, feeling they demean the transcendence of the Almighty God. To be honest, their fears are often fulfilled in those who feign a chumminess with God that distorts who he really is.

But we must not let an abuse of others keep us from the real thing God offers us. As we shall see finding a true friendship with the Living God never demeans who he is. It doesn't reduce him to our level and allow us to treat him tritely; it only defines his Fatherhood in ever-more grandeur.

The fact that my earthly father extends to me his friendship does not diminish his fatherhood. It only defines it more clearly. Just because I'm his friend, doesn't mean I don't also give him respect as my father. He wants us to so trust his love so that we can be secure in his presence. But it is still the presence of the Living God, which makes this friendship all that much more incredible.

To experience it, however, we need to appreciate just how much we are loved. That isn't easy for a generation of believers who have been invited to know him, not because he is so overwhelmingly wonderful, but because we were scared to death by the threat of an eternity in hell.

I no longer call you servants, because a servant does not know his master's business. Instead, I have called you friends, for everything that I learned from my Father I have made known to you.

—JOHN 15:15

For your personal journey

Spend a few moments thinking about your relationship with God. Do you see it growing in closeness and sensitivity, or does it feel abstract? Is he more real than your closest friend, or a distant presence that rarely seems to engage the real issues of your life? If your relationship with him isn't what you want it to be, ask him to help you grow to know him better and to recognize his presence throughout each day.

Threatened With Hell

"The Satanic assumption is that men and women cannot love God for his own sake."
DAVID BOAN AND JOHN YATES IN AN UNPUBLISHED MANUSCRIPT

The question is compelling. "Do you know where you would end up if you died in a car accident tonight?"

The evangelist has already painted the pictures. You could find yourself in an eternal garden of exquisite beauty laced together with winding paths of gold; or, writhing in agony amidst the leaping sulfuric flames of hell.

If there was ever a choice that defined "no-brainer," this is it. Once you convince someone that hell and heaven exist winning a convert is easy. After all, praying for forgiveness and "accepting Jesus" seem like a small price to pay for a "Get-Out-of-Hell-Free Card!"

So effective is this appeal to people's worst fears and insecurities that hell has become the most popular invitation into God's kingdom. What we have not so critically examined is whether or not threatening people with hell engages them in the relationship God has always wanted with them.

For we live in a day when millions of people have made a commitment to Christ and yet so few lives are really transformed by his power. It has been said of this generation that our Christianity is a mile wide but only an inch deep. We see effects of it everywhere. People claim to know God, but show no evidence of transformation in their daily lives. We challenge them as hypocrites and attempt to badger them into more righteous lifestyles, but in the end most believers end up as much a part of the world's ways as their nonbelieving neighbors.

While the threat of hell can stir instant commitments, it is not breeding long-term disciples. If you are only in this kingdom because you fear the alternative, you've missed the greatest part of what it means to know God.

WHY THE THREAT?

No one ever threatened me to do something that was wonderful to do. My parents didn't threaten me with punishment to get me to go to Disneyland. But to make me go to the dentist or work on the vineyard, that was another matter.

So if I am told that I must love God or he will throw me into hell, I might well consider loving him—or at least pretend I do. But if the only reason I'm even responding to him is to serve my own self-interest and escape a fiery eternity in hell, am I really loving him or myself?

Can a true friendship blossom under so grave a threat? Let's say I approach a recent acquaintance of mine, hoping to deepen our friendship. I say to him, "I have really appreciated the time we've been able to spend together. In fact, I'd like to see our relationship deepen and maybe even become best friends. How would you like to spend some time together over the next few months and see if that kind of friendship develops?"

So far, so good! But what if I added one more sentence? "I

hope you do, because if you don't, I'm going to hunt you down and torture you for the rest of your life." Hasn't the invitation just taken an ominous turn? Even if he wanted to explore the potential of a friendship with me, it has now been twisted by my threat. What does it say about me, and how will he ever feel safe in a friendship cultivated on fear?

Whether you are conscious of it or not, the threat of hell can create an inner dissonance in our perception of the God who seeks our love. How can we feel safe with a God who is seemingly anxious to dangle us over the flames of hell? If he can find nothing else to call us to come to him, then what kind of God must he be? And if we can find no better reason to love him, how shallow must our faith be?

A recent full-page advertisement for Evangelism Explosion in a popular Christian leadership journal quoted a popular television preacher: "If God would dip all pastors in hell for a fraction of a second and then yank them up by their shirttails—as they are standing there smoldering and their clothes and skin are full of black soot, and their shoes have half melted off, I think their commitment to the Great Commission would substantially increase."

Sadly, he's probably right, but that may point more to our weakness than God's intentions. The threat of hell may get people to evangelize more, to repeat a sinner's prayer or even join a congregation, but in doing so it a sordid view of God as one who delights in searing the soles of our shoes in order to get us to do things his way. Such a view of him will not invite us into the depths of his love.

CONTRADICTORY PORTRAITS?

Here is the problem, isn't it? Scripture seems to paint two contradictory portraits of the Living God—a terrible judge and a loving Father. Which is it? Can he be both?

We read not only that God has prepared hell for the unbelieving, but also that he commanded Joshua to practice ethnic cleansing in Canaan, poured out fire from heaven to consume Sodom and Gomorrah and opened the earth to swallow those who opposed Moses. Unapproachable in his purity, even the most righteous fell on their faces near his presence paralyzed by their unworthiness. He demanded unquestioning obedience and punished with unspeakable anguish those who did not comply.

No wonder we're at least a little confused when he appears in the New Testament telling us how much he loves us and inviting us to be his children. We see Jesus healing the sick, forgiving prostitutes and murderers, going into the houses of sinners. He invited children in his lap and portrayed his Father as so tender that the most wayward sinner could run to his side in absolute safety.

So what happened to God? Did he get saved somewhere between Malachi and Matthew? Had he reinvented himself into a nicer, gentler God? Of course not! He is unchanging, the same throughout all eternity.

So, then is he both? Is he kind and gentle to those who please him, and vengeful toward the wicked? That's what many of us have been taught to think, which is why we end up playing he-loves-me-he-loves-me-not games. We sift through every event to try and figure out if we are in his favor or out of it. If we think we are in, we can relax and coast through life. If, however, we think our difficulties prove we are out of favor then we have to try harder to please him; a course of action, Paul warns us against. True righteousness cannot come from human effort.

There's the problem. I can't please him until I'm certain of his love for me, but he will not love me if I cannot please him. This is an endless loop that offers no resolution. How can he be a mean and vengeful God one moment and a kind and tender one the next. Those portraits don't depict the same God in different circumstances, but rather contradictory portraits that leave us confused and uncertain of God's true nature.

Unless we can glean from Scripture a cohesive view of God's nature we'll never know who he really is or have the confidence to embrace the relationship he desires with us. God did not change between Malachi and Matthew. Our perception of him, however, changed drastically.

Before Jesus came we could only see God's actions and assume he was moved by motivations similar to our own. His actions against sin made him appear as if he didn't care for people. His attempts to teach his people to trust him were misunderstood as vengeful punishment.

Jesus changed all of that. By listening to his words and watching how he lived we suddenly see God's motivations. He fully reflected the Father's glory so we might know him as he really is and no longer be victims of our own misinterpretations. Love dwells at the core of God's being, and the Old Testament contains hundreds of pictures of a God who is rich in mercy, willing to forgive, and passionate about setting us free from the sin that diminishes and devours the life he wants us to experience in him.

He allows us the consequences of sin, not because he delights in our anguish, but so that we can see its devastating effects and run to the only one in the universe who can set us free from them. His wrath against sin was not his rejection of us in anger, but only a reflection of the depth of his love that cannot look away unconcerned as sin destroys us.

These are not mere philosophical issues. If we aren't certain of God's motives towards us, we will never have confidence to engage his presence in the reality of our lives. We'll keep him at a safe distance and miss what he desires most for us the—a friendship with him more real and more powerful than any we've known before.

"DO I HAVE TO?"

Those who seek to follow God only because they don't want to go to hell, never discover how incredible a Father he really is. They see Christianity as an onerous burden and don't want to do one bit more than they absolutely must.

I've heard the question literally hundreds of times. Struggling with sin, or desiring something that Scripture marks out of bounds for the believer, they'll ask what I think they should do. When I tell them what Scripture seems to say, I see the look in their eye—gears turning hoping to find a loophole so they can still have what they desire and not end up in hell.

From the lips of a woman wanting to marry a man who

doesn't share her faith, "Do I have to, to be saved?"

From the angry man who doesn't want to forgive the person who cheated him, "Do I have to, to be saved?"

From the person who wants to justify the habit God wants to free him from, "Do I have to, in order to be saved?"

How does one answer that question? If you say yes, then you emptied the cross of its power by substituting human effort. If you say no, they will use it as an excuse to indulge themselves in a false notion of what it means to live in God.

I finally discovered that the question itself is unfair, and shows how far removed Christianity has become from its central purpose. Instead of desiring to walk in friendship with him, we are only preoccupied with securing his goodies. It's his blessing we want not him! How painful that must be for him.

It would be as if I invited my adult son over to dinner some Friday evening. He hesitates a moment. It's obvious he'd rather not come, but before he answers he wants to know one thing: "Dad, I guess I could come but I've got other things I'd like to do. Will you write me out of your will if I don't come?"

What answer can a father give to that question? None would really suffice, since the question misses the whole point of relationship. True, God has the best goodies in all the universe, but the person who seeks those without desiring to know him misses out on the real life of the kingdom.

That's what people are saying who wonder if they must do something or risk losing their salvation. They don't want one drop more of God's life than the minimum required to escape hell. How tragic! No wonder they missed the best gift God could give them, and why Jesus wanted so desperately to free them from the tyranny of trying to earn eternal life by their own religious efforts.

All this is not to say that hell does not exist, nor that those who refuse God won't end up there. Scripture is remarkably clear on that point. What I am saying is that when we use the threat of hell to motivate people to come to God, we are using it in a way Jesus never did and in a way he never intended. In doing so, we push people further away from God's greatest desire, not invite them closer to it.

His message was not, come to God or you'll burn in hell. His message was that God's kingdom has come near you and you can become a participant in it. You have a Father who loves you like no other father you've ever known in your life and can now discover what it means to have a daily relationship with him. If not, then your own sin will destroy you utterly and completely.

Jesus compared this life to a treasure discovered in a field; something so valuable that you would give up anything to possess it. His life is not something you have to follow. He is worth knowing just because of how incredibly awesome he is. If you only want his gifts without wanting him you cheat yourself out of the best portion.

Here the fear of hell is no use to us at all. The insecurity it breeds only takes us further from him and makes us uncertain about who he is. Jesus wanted us to be very clear about who his Father is because we only grow in him to the degree that we trust his love for us.

There will be no one in hell that he did not love with all his heart. His love reaches to every person across every sin and failure, hoping that at some moment they will come to know just how loved they are.

There is nothing more important for you to know.

The kingdom of heaven is like treasure hidden in a field.
When a man found it, he hid it again, and then in his joy
went and sold all he had and bought that field.
—MATTHEW 13:44

√ √ √

For your personal journey

Did you come to God only because you were afraid of the alternative or were you entreated by his love? Do you view him as a stern judge, or as a loving Father? If the former, ask God to reveal himself to you as he really is. Over the next few week look for ways God will help you let go of your fears and let his love capture your heart as your sole motivation for walking after him.

A Father Like No Other

If we take all the goodness, wisdom and compassion of the best mothers and fathers who have ever lived, they would only be a faint shadow of the love and mercy in the heart of the redeeming God.
—BRENNAN MANNING IN *THE SIGNATURE OF JESUS*

"The old man is a fool! And so is my brother. Good riddance to you all!"

If those weren't his words, they at least express his attitude. How he must have cackled in delight that his father had actually given him his share of the inheritance that he had demanded it. He was finally free of his father and the hard work the family farm, too. With more money than he could imagine spending in a lifetime, he walked off to find himself in a world filled with opportunity.

All didn't go as he planned. How quickly his excessive pleasures devoured his money. Then when a severe famine swept his adopted country, he had to use what was left just to survive. But even that ran out eventually and he had to sell himself into slavery to a master who fed his livestock better than his servants.

One day he found himself coveting the slop tossed to the pigs, and only then did he think of home again. This time he did not loathe it, he longed for it. He had been better off at home. He wondered if it would be possible to go back there again.

Traditionally this story is called "The Parable of the Prodigal Son" and is one of Jesus' most poignant tales. It has been told and retold, because it is so easy to identify with the son and the mercy he received in spite of his arrogance and stupidity.

By calling it the Prodigal Son, however, we lose the central focus of the parable. He was only one of two brothers, each dealing with an estrangement from their father, albeit in vastly different ways.

The central character is the father himself and for that reason I wish it were called the "Parable of the Incredible Father." For Jesus used this story to paint a portrait of his Father, and believe me, this is like no father you've ever known.

WHAT FATHER IS THIS?

Anyone hearing Jesus' story for the first time would be shocked at this father's actions. His arrogant son dishonors him by asking for his inheritance while the father is still alive, and who by all indications is nowhere near death's door. What kind of son claims his father's inheritance while he's still alive? How dare he even ask!

As rude as the son's request might be, we can at least understand it. We all know what it is to want to get our hands on dad's money, even if most of us are too civil to pursue it. But it's this father who defies comprehension.

What does the father do in response to this outrageous request? *He gives it to him.*

This is even more shocking than the son asking. He divides the inheritance between his two sons and lets him go. How many fathers would do that, especially when they knew the younger son was up to no good?

What kind of father is this?

The son squanders his inheritance on his own pleasure, instead of investing it for the future. But the father does not go and nag him. He finally loses it all and ends up destitute. But the father does not try to rescue him. Where is the father? He is back on the farm, waiting. He doesn't chase after his son to tell him that he's foolish nor does he rush off to buy him dinner when famine hits. He waits.

What kind of father is this?

Is he indifferent to his son's plight? Any parent who has ever watched their son or daughter make bad choices, knows that waiting is far more difficult than prodding or nagging. But wait he does, for a marvelous thing to happen—to let the son come to his senses.

We soon find out, however, just how expectant that waiting was. Years later when he returns the father spots him while he is still a long ways off. The only way that would have happened was if the father had been constantly looking. He probably never walked by the road without looking down it, hoping against hope that today would be the day his boy would come home. I can see him with one eye on his work, the other focused down the road, looking for the familiar gait of his beloved son. One day he spots him, even though he would have been emaciated with hunger and hunched over in humiliation. "That's him! That's my boy!"

What does he do now? Does he stand on the porch with arms crossed waiting for his son to walk all the way to the house humiliated, then fall down in the dirt and grovel for his next meal? That's what I might have done. I would even have practiced my I-hope-you-learned-your-lesson speech. Not this father.

Without hesitation the father jumps off the porch and runs down the road. This is all the more amazing when you remember how this father would have been dressed. He wouldn't have been wearing pants or jogging shorts, but long, cumbersome robes. In that time it was dishonorable for an older man to run, exposing his legs in the process. But this father again demonstrates his love by sacrificing his own dignity in deference to his son. He hiked up his robes and went barreling down the road as fast as he could run.

What kind of father is this?

Can you imagine what his son must have thought when he finally looked up and saw his father bearing down on him? Could he tell if he was joyful or angry? He must have thought the latter, for he launches into his prepared speech even before his father gets there. "I am no longer worthy to be called your son; make me like one of your hired men."

But his words are not even acknowledged by the father, as he reaches his son and swallows up the words with hugs and kisses of delight. Not a hint of anger comes from the father, nor would he talk one moment about his offer to be his servant. He was too overcome with joy; the son he'd always wanted had found his way home.

Moments later the father's servants arrive. They must have seen him running down the road and chased after him, anxious to see what the father would do to his selfish son. What a shock it must have been for them to come upon such a festival of celebration. The father turns to them too. "Get a robe, a ring, and a new pair of sandals. Stoke up the fire and let's get ready to celebrate."

A party? For the son that squandered the family inheritance on his own selfish pleasures? How could this be? The son deserved punishment not a party!

What kind of father is this?

WHAT THE FATHER WANTED MOST

Isn't it amazing how at each point in the story this father acts completely the opposite of how we would expect a loving father to act?

He should never have given him an early inheritance, especially not to such an irresponsible son. He shouldn't have stood by while his son wasted away. And certainly he shouldn't have welcomed him home so extravagantly without making him pay for his stupidity. His actions make no sense at all, unless he wanted something more for his son than mere responsible behavior.

Though it may appear that what the son wanted drove this story, a closer look shows just otherwise. What the Father wanted is the key here, and he wanted it so desperately he would spare nothing to have it. What do you think that was? Was it to be with his sons or to have them labor in his fields? No, the story started there and he could easily have kept the younger one there by refusing his request and giving him no opportunity to make such a wreak of his life. That wasn't enough for this father. He wanted something more.

What he didn't have was a loving relationship with either of his sons. The younger son only saw him as a conduit to his own pleasures; the elder as a taskmaster to serve in the fields. They were both in the house, but neither was at home in his love. Could that be why the father let the younger son go? Rather than force him to stay and deepen his hostility, he let him go to run to the end of his own self-sufficiency and find out who his father really was.

For it is at that moment when he looks with longing at the food given to the pigs that he realizes his father is a much kinder man than the farmer he's working for now. It's then that he comes to his senses and decides to go home. But he still has no idea what kind of father he's about to meet. Afraid of his anger, embarrassed by the mess he made of his life, he prepared a speech, confessing his unworthiness to be considered a son.

Even then he had no idea how loved he was, and that nothing he had done in the intervening years had compromised that love.

This father wanted an intimate friendship with both of his children. He wanted them to know how deeply they were loved and to experience their love in return. He didn't want his sons' obedience, but their hearts. Knowing it would only come when the son truly understood who his father really was, he risked it all by letting the son have what he wanted. Only by coming to the end of himself, would he come to recognize what had been important to the father all along.

As a parent of adult children, I understand that easily. There's nothing I prize more with my children than those moments when we share the honesty and intimacy of friendship. When they know I love them, and they respond the same way to me, there's nothing better.

That's the point of Jesus' story. The father was not manipulating the son by anything he did. He was only loving the son at the deepest possible level. That love explains why the father let him go in the first place and why he rushed so hard to embrace him. He knew his son's sin had been punishment enough. He ran because he didn't want his son to hurt one second longer than was absolutely necessary. His pain had brought him home. Nothing else mattered.

God feels the same way about you. He's not interested in your service or sacrifice. He only wants you to know how much you are loved, hoping that you will choose to love him in return. Understand that and everything else about your life will fall into place; miss that and nothing else will make any difference.

LIVING LESS-LOVED

In this incredible story, when do you think the father loved his son the most?

Every time I share this story I ask people that question. Almost always the first answers select the moment where the father meets the son on the road. After a bit more thought, however, some suggest it might be when the father gives him his inheritance and lets him go. Only then does it become clear: there is no point in the story where the father loved his son more than at any other point. He loved him completely through the whole process. It is the only constant in the story.

The events in this story cannot be accounted for by the varying love of the father—only the varying perception of it by the son. Though he was not less-loved at any point in the story, through most of it he lives as if he was.

When he took the money from his father and stormed off the farm grateful to be out from under his clutches and free to pursue his own way, he lived less-loved.

When he spent this money in a foreign land, wasting it on his own pleasures and thinking he'd finally fooled his father, he lived less-loved.

Even when he started for home practicing his plea of repentance, willing only to be a slave to a father who had sought a son, he lived less-loved.

But finally, when he's home in the robe, the sandals, and the ring , sitting at his father's table sinking his teeth into the filet mignon, it finally sinks in. He is loved. But he always was! It's just that now he can stop living as if he wasn't.

Most of our lives are spent living less-loved.

When we worry that God will ask us for some horrible sacrifice, we live less-loved.

When we indulge ourselves in sin, we live less-loved.

When we give into anxiety in the crush of our circumstances, we live less-loved.

When we try to earn God's favor by our own efforts, we live less-loved.

Even when we get caught up in religious obligations to make ourselves acceptable to him, we live less-loved.

That is the story of the older brother. At the end of the story he is so angry at his father for receiving his wayward brother home, he refuses to come to the house and join the celebration. He had stayed with his father, never having run off to pursue his own aims, but still missed out on the relationship his father wanted with him. Though a son, he saw himself only as a slave and every request of his father as an onerous chore.

The first son represents those who run from God by indulging their own selfish pursuits; the older son represents those who work hard to impress God with their commitment. Fearful of the consequences of not doing so, they slave away for him. But they never come to the depth of relationship the Father wants with them. The Pharisees in Jesus' day were like that as are many people today who are caught up in a host of religious activities, but miss out on what it really means to live in the Father's love.

In the long run it doesn't matter whether rebellion or religion keep you from a vibrant relationship with the Father, the result is still the same. He is cheated out of the relationship he wants with you, and you never come to know how he feels about you.

Jesus ends the story at an interesting point. The younger son is in the house enjoying his new-found relationship with his father. The older son is still outside weighing his options. Will he come to know just how much he is loved and join the celebration, or will he remain convinced of his father's unfairness and remain outside angry and alone?

The choice is his—and it is yours! Everything about your life hinges on the answer to one simple question.

Do you know how loved you really are?

Isn't it about time you found out?

> *And I pray that you, being rooted and established in love, may have power, together with all the saints, to grasp how wide and long and high and deep is the love of Christ, and to know this love that surpasses knowledge— that you may be filled to the measure of all the fullness of God.*
>
> —EPHESIANS 3:17-19

For your personal journey

Ask God to show you where you live less-loved. What does it make you do—run to your own way like the younger brother or work even harder like the older one? God wants you to know that there is nothing you can do to make him love you any more today, and nothing you can do that will make him love you any less. He just loves you. Ask him to teach you how true that is so you can live in freedom.

Welcome Home

"The great danger facing all of us...is that some day we may wake up and find that we have been busy with husks and trappings of life and have really missed life itself. That is what one prays one's friends may be spared — satisfaction with a life that...has in it no tingle or thrill that comes from a friendship with the Father."
PHILLIPS BROOKS (1835-1893) *SERMONS*

I've seen that look at least a dozen times. Should I trust or should I not?

I know well the battle that rages not fifteen yards from me as the latest stray puppy tries to decide whether I'm safe or not. The torment is unbearable. She makes a few halting steps forward, then thinks better and turns her head away as if to break a spell about to overcome her. I would love to rush in, scoop her off her feet and convince her how safe she is, but if I so much as lean forward, she scurries even further into the darkness. Right now, the dog across from me has no idea what awaits her if she can overcome her fear.

All the benefits of my house are hers if she comes, and they are considerable. The long list of stray or abandoned puppies that have showed up in our front yard, make me wonder if our address isn't scratched on a fire hydrant somewhere because my wife must be the softest touch in town when it comes to a dog without a home.

Here strays receive the royal treatment—complete with a flea bath, loving attention and plenty of food and water. Over the next week my wife will do everything she can to locate the owner if it was lost. Failing that she will take an ad out in the newspaper promising a free puppy to a good home and will only let it go when she's convinced the new family will treat her puppy well.

Many warm up to the attention right away, but others act as if they've been beaten by every human they've ever known. Instead of running toward the open gate, the lighted doorway, and all the love they could handle, they shrink back in the shadows unsure whether it's safe.

The latest puppy is one of those. I hold out my hand, offering her food. I know she hasn't eaten in awhile because I can count every rib right through her fur. I coax lovingly, speaking in soft tones, trying to caress her with my words. The game will continue for awhile. I will not force her into my home, and allow her fears to be a risk to my children and my dogs. If she comes, she'll have to come willingly.

The game will go one for awhile and right now it could go either way. Will I take care of her and help her, or will I be like all the others who have hurt or abandoned her? She doesn't want any more pain, preferring to leave now if my invitation will only add more grief.

I know exactly how she feels. Every time I play this game, I can't help but think how much this mirrors God's entreaty to me, and the difficult time I have learning to trust him. The choice to trust is never easy—not for stray dogs, nor for stray sons and daughters.

A PLACE PREPARED

"In my Father's house are many rooms; if it were not so, I would have told you. I am going there to prepare a place for you. And if I go and prepare a place for you, I will

*come back and take you to be with me that you also may
be where I am.*"

—JOHN 14:2-3

Could the invitation be any clearer? Jesus told his followers
about a house, with a Father who waits for them to come and
take their place in his home. Does this sound familiar?

We so easily miss the point of his words when we mistakenly
relegate them to the distant future, of a second coming and man-
sions in heaven. Here Jesus was still talking about his first 'going
away'—his death on a cross; and his first 'coming back'—the resurrection. These events would unfold in the next few days and
Jesus wanted them to understand just how important they were.

The cross stands as the pivotal event in opening the door for
us to dwell in the Father's Love. The apostle Paul told us than *then*
when we really understand what happened there between a
Father and a Son we would know for certain and forever just
how deep their love is for us. Later on we'll take a look from
this vantage point at the power of the cross.

He was going to open a door, and return after the
Resurrection to show them how to live in his Father's house—
the place in Father's heart he's prepared for each one of them.

The disciples, however, couldn't make sense of his words.
When he told them they knew the way where he was going,
Thomas challenged him. "We don't know where you are going,
so how can we know the way?"

"You know me, Philip and I am the way."

He knew they were confused. He knew they didn't understand the new relationship they would be able to have with him
and his Father after the Resurrection. But he says it simply—you
know me! I will get you there. Notice how he focuses here not
on the process they would have to follow, but on the person they
would need to know. He takes it right back to relationship
again. "Stay with me; you'll know everything you need to know."

A FATHER YOU CAN TRUST

To have the relationship God desires with you, and for

which your heart must cry out or you still wouldn't be reading this book, you simply have to learn to trust him.

I know that is far easier to talk about than it is to do. We've learned all our lives that trusting other people will only leave us frustrated and disappointed. Even the people who might have loved us the most probably failed us at some point. The lesson our flesh teaches us from a very young age is take care of yourself, because no one else will.

Perhaps like some of the strays who come to our house, everyone you've ever trusted has betrayed that trust. Maybe you even feel that God has betrayed your trust when he didn't do things for you that you thought a loving father would do. If the truth be told many of us have been exploited by people who came to us in God's name, claiming to know God's will for us, who only wanted to exploit us to meet their own needs.

My heart goes out most of all to those whose earthly fathers betrayed their trust and whose past is marred by failure and brokenness. I know some of you reading this book, keep doing so because the message stirs you. But every time you read the word *Father* something cringes inside of you. It's not a term of endearment to you, but one that scratches at old wounds.

For you, *Father* only conjures images of abuse or abandonment. It amazes me that so many who hunger to know God had fathers who were so broken they couldn't even reflect the smallest hint of his love to their own children. Either selfishly seeking their own pleasure, or using you as a punching bags for their own pain, they left a wake of wounded children who don't know what it is to have a father.

Betrayal by the people we most want to love us can leave deep scars. But even these are not beyond God's ability to heal and redeem. In fact, the reason those wounds hurt so deeply is because God created us to be loved by a Father that puts even the best earthly examples to shame. Even those of us who had good fathers, can't imagine how much greater a father he really is. Even the best fathers, as we saw in the last chapter, can't hold a candle to the love the Eternal Father has in his heart for you.

It may take awhile, but God can help us not define his fatherhood based on the failed record of broken humanity, but let his fatherhood define what it really is to be loved by the most awesome Father in the universe.

So even if the word *father* doesn't convey the most tender image to you, please don't write yourself out of his house. Learning to trust him is the most difficult thing any of us will ever learn to do. If I can understand that for a stray puppy cowering in my front yard, how much more does the Father of heaven and earth understand our wounds and our insecurities.

With incredible patience and love, he coaxes us out of our fears to embrace him. He waits for that moment when suddenly we know we are safer in him than in any other place we could be. It may be timidly at first, but turn toward him and abandon yourselves to trust him in the smallest way you can.

He understands how afraid you are that you'll be disappointed once again. But he's still there patiently extending his hand to you. He will try to get closer, until you cower away in fear. Then he will back off so as not add to your pain, hoping his gentleness will one day win you over.

ONLY TRUST HIM

Trust. It is so easy to talk about, but so hard to put into practice. Nothing is more theologically certain than that God is faithful and trustworthy. But learning how to live in that trust through the twists and turns of our lives is the most difficult challenge we face.

It took God almost Abraham's entire life to teach Abraham the joy of trusting him. But he did it. Even when he was asked to give up his only son and heir, he trusted God's plan and God's nature enough to set about the task. This, from the one who had risked his wife's virtue by lying to Pharaoh that she was not his wife. This, from the one who had impregnated his wife's maidservant when it didn't appear God would give Sarah the child he promised.

To accomplish that, God did some extraordinary things for Abraham. Rest assured, God knows how difficult it is for you to trust him. He is not threatened by that nor angry with you.

He simply wants you to keep your eye on him and learn.

He knows that only by trusting him can you participate in relationship with him and enjoy the fullness of life in his household. He also knows that you'll trust him only to the degree that your certain of his love for you.

This is why he created you and why he designed such an extraordinary plan to teach you exactly how to lay aside your fears and walk into his arms. Then he can scoop you up, hold you closely to himself and fulfill what began in his heart for you since before the creation of the world.

This is the journey of a lifetime—to trust him more and more everyday for the rest of our lives. The more we trust him, the more of his life we can experience. But don't try to do this on your own. You don't have it in you. He can take you by the hand and teach you just how much you are loved so that you no longer have to pursue your own way and protect yourself in ways that only seem to backfire, hurting you and others around you.

NICE GOD OR MEAN GOD?

We had just completed a spirited discussion on God's grace from Paul's letter to the Galatians at a men's retreat in the Sierra Nevada mountains. A young man had been waiting to talk with me for some time until enough people cleared out so we could talk privately.

"Over these two days I've listened to you talk about God as a loving Father. Since I became a Christian I have only served a mean God, fearful every day that I might miss his will and be rejected. I really want to believe he is the incredible Father you speak about, but I've decided not to."

"Really?" I asked. "Why is that?"

"I'm just not sure you're right. I've thought about this over the last day or so and I've made a decision. I'm going to keep serving the mean God." He had it all worked out. "The way I figure it, If I'm right and serve the mean God, then I'll be fine on judgment day. If I'm wrong and he is the Father you're talking about, he will understand why I did what I did.

"But if I change now and serve this loving Father, what happens if he turns out to be the mean God I've always thought him to be? Then I'm in trouble."

"Certainly, that's your choice," I told him. "But before you do, can I ask you a question?"

"What's that?"

"Would the God you're serving ever trade his life on a cross for yours?"

He looked up at me and shook his head. "No way!"

"Then how can he be the God of Bible?"

God knew it wouldn't be easy for us to accept such an incredible offer of friendship, which is why he went to such lengths to convince us."

I was only with him for a weekend and I don't know how he has walked it out since, but he is like so many others I've met along the journey. Out of the dissonant portraits of God they have decided that it is safer to treat him as the mean God.

They don't have any idea just how wrong they are.

And they don't know that fearing a demanding God, will never take them into the house. They will never be able to do enough to earn what he wants to give them.

To enter the house we must trade our fear of him for a love that is far stronger.

> Come to me, all you who are weary and burdened, and I will give you rest. Take my yoke upon you and learn from me, for I am gentle and humble in heart, and you will find rest for your souls.
> —MATTHEW 11:29

For your personal journey

What reservations do you have about entrusting yourself completely to God? Realize that the only way to grow in trust is to grow in the knowledge of his love. Ask him every day to reveal the depth of his love to you and in doing so teach you how to trust him more.

What Fear Could Never Achieve

There is no fear in love.
But perfect love drives out fear, because
fear has to do with punishment. The one who fears
is not made perfect in love.

—1 John 4:18

6

The Tyranny of the Favor Line

"God is good. You are bad. Try harder!"
THE OBSERVATIONS OF A FIFTEEN-YEAR-OLD
SUMMING UP AN EVENING WITH HER YOUTH GROUP

W ho could blame the young mother? I certainly couldn't?

She was in her early thirties, the mother of two children. I don't even remember the congenital disease her youngest child had, but at six years of age he was already confined to a wheelchair. Often his parents rushed him to the hospital in such critical condition that they were never sure if they would bring him home again.

Every time I was with them, I was touched not only by the depth of their need but also the sweetness with which they seemed to endure it. They had grown up in Christian homes and had sought to follow God faithfully into their adult years. I often prayed for them and their child, hoping he would some day be healed.

I had no idea, however, that the stress of his illness was also shredding their marriage until I called one morning after I had not seen them for a few weeks. I found a devastated mother on the other end of the phone. Her husband had left her two weeks before, and she now had sole responsibility for their sick boy.

Overwhelmed with pain, she told me that she was no longer sure God even existed, or if he did that he was not the God she had thought him to be. Not only had six years of praying for her son's healing proved fruitless, but the need had also destroyed her marriage. She was alone, disillusioned and angry.

I tried to tell her that God still loved her and cared about her needs, but she rebuffed my encouragement. "Do you have any idea what it is like not to be able to ever just relax and enjoy your own child, because you are never sure that he will be there tomorrow?"

I told her honestly that I did not. I only had a brief taste of anything similar. Our first-born daughter had a severe case of jaundice, and I remember how resentful I felt having to take her for a daily blood test and watch my baby scream in pain as they drew it from her toes. That lasted only a week and her life was never in jeopardy. How do you multiply that by six years of standing at death's door with your little boy?

I did offer to help her with whatever resources we had to get her through the days ahead, but she declined. "I just can't keep living this way," she sobbed. "Whatever God expects of me, I just don't have it to give."

Rarely in my life have I felt as inadequate as I did the moment I placed the phone back in its cradle. After nearly fifteen years of pastoral ministry, I didn't have the answers she needed. Only later did I learn why. At the time I was caught in the same trap she was, only on the other side of it. She thought her overwhelming need pointed to her faithlessness and loss of favor with God while I thought my more pleasant circumstances were proof that I had been faithful and thus had earned his favor.

We were both living under the tyranny of the favor line. She was already paying for it; I was about to.

THE FAVOR LINE

What is the favor line? It's that invisible line that tells us whether or not we've met enough of someone's expectations to merit their approval. It's impossible to live in this world without recognizing its impact on every area of life.

Our parents had one. We knew what made them proud of us, and what brought their displeasure or even anger. If your parents expectations were fair you could play the favor line, acting especially kind when you wanted something from them, or hiding behind their back what you knew would merit punishment. If your parents expectations were unreasonable, then maybe you grew up without any approval at all.

We found the same favor line when we went to school, though it existed there in a graduated scale. The higher expectations we met, the better grade we received and the greater approval from teachers and parents.

It didn't take us long to discover that our friends had favor lines as well to derive the benefits of their friendship. Disappoint them however, and our so-called friends could turn on us in a heartbeat; as we would on them. We found the same line in the work world as well. Those who achieved or exceeded expectations found themselves in the bosses' good graces, with all the perks that favor brought.

We've learned to survive in this world by currying favor where we needed it, so it is only natural to assume that God has a favor line as well.

As long as our circumstances are pleasant, or even bearable, we may not think much about God's favor. But, let trouble or disappointment encroach on our quiet existence and we begin to wonder how God feels about us. Does he love me? Have I offended him? Am I doing enough for him to like me? Struggling with those questions brings us right back to the favor line as we look for some way to get back on God's good side.

King David expressed so eloquently how the favor line superimposes itself on our pursuit of God:

"LORD, who may dwell in your sanctuary? Who may

live on your holy hill? He whose walk is blameless and
who does what is righteous, who speaks the truth from
his heart and has no slander on his tongue..."
—PSALM 15:1-3a

He continues with a list of traits that qualify people to come before the Holy God. Other lists in Scripture seem to underline his assertion—the Ten Commandments, the Great Commission, the fruits of the Spirit just to name a few. It is easy to see why people who seriously pursue God end up with a favor line drawn across their lives and why they think they can assess at any moment how God feels about them by whether they are living above or below it.

Bible reading, prayer, church involvement, and helping others seem to put us above the line. Selfish motives or sinful actions push us beneath it. That would seem easy enough, except that we're never sure how much of any of these things actually matter.

I've asked audiences all over the world, "How many of you think that you pray enough? Read the Bible enough? Or, witness enough?" I've never gotten so much as one person to raise a hand to my query.

I know what they are thinking, because I've thought it too. How much is enough, after all? If I pray an hour a day, couldn't I as easily do two? If I read two chapters a day, should I be reading four? Do I need to witness once a month, once a week, to every stranger I meet?

In the same way we know in our more genuine moments that we are not entirely free of sin. We may be able to hide it well enough, but thoughts, motives and hidden deeds all expose our ongoing struggle with sin and doubt. Can we ever be sure how much of our failures God is willing to overlook as part of our maturing process?

That's why I call it the tyranny of the favor line. Trying to live under the weight of David's list, or anyone else's, would disqualify everyone of us from God's presence and his favor. If you've tried it you know how hard it is to do everything you think he requires. The only way to feel good about it is when you think you're at least doing more than other believers around you. But you know intrinsically that you'll never be good enough.

This problem is compounded whenever we encounter difficult or painful circumstances. Who doesn't wonder at such times if we're being punished for not being good enough? We joke about it in the most trivial things, such as getting stopped at consecutive stop lights. "Wow, you must not be living right," someone invariably observes.

But it's no joking matter when we suddenly lose a job or face a life-threatening disease. The tyranny of the favor line is unrelenting, never allowing us to be certain about how God feels about us. So we're left to pick through our circumstances: *He loves me! He loves me not!*

A FAR BETTER PLAN

Is it any wonder then, that my young friend would sum up the ministry of her youth group by saying, "Same old thing, Dad. God is good. You are bad. Try harder!" Unfortunately too many people think that's the essence of the gospel and yet on that basis none of us could ever stand before him.

Even David knew that in his more desperate moments. As he hid in a cave from those who sought to kill him, he cried out for God's mercy. "Do not bring your servant into judgment, for no one living is righteous before you" (Psalm 143:2). Aware of his own weaknesses, he was not willing to stake God's favor on his performance.

Later, as he prostrated himself over the public exposure of his adultery and the murder of the cheated husband and as he grieved the loss of the son his affair produced, he again seeks another standard. "The sacrifices of God are a broken spirit; a broken and contrite heart, O God, you will not despise" (Psalm 51:17).

The truth of the matter is that the same Scriptures that give us lists of qualifications to earn God's favor, also clearly state that there is not enough goodness in any one of us to fulfill those requirements. Only Jesus would be able to do so. No matter how much we try to earn his favor we will always fall short. The more effort we give, the more distant he will seem.

Why? Because the favor line causes us to swing between periods of self-pity and self-righteousness. When we recognize our shortcomings, we want to give up in despair. But even when we feel good about our efforts, we cannot understand why God doesn't make himself as real for us as Scripture seems to indicate he wants to. Self-righteousness can be a far greater deterrent to the relationship God wants with us than our failures and mistakes.

When our best-intentioned efforts go unrewarded, we may become disillusioned and drift away. For great periods of time we find ourselves distracted from even thinking about our relationship with God and try to satiate our hunger with a host of other things—our work, other people, religious services or even buying new things. Though these may work for awhile, in quieter moments the hunger returns. None of these things will ever satisfy the hunger that longs to know the Living God.

That's why trying to live to the favor line will at some point leave you stranded in hopelessness. Either like Peter, after he denied Jesus on the night he needed him most, you will be disillusioned by your own failure to do the good you know to do; or like Job you will question whether or not God even loves you or treats you fairly.

God never wanted us to end up in either place. He instead invites us not to walk the tightrope of the favor line, but discover a far better way to know him.

AN INCREDIBLE SURPRISE

At a young age he had already advanced well beyond his peers. Educated in the best schools, he was recognized as one of the most influential religious leaders in one of the best-known cities of the world. His morals were impeccable and his wisdom knew no equal.

But all was not as well on the inside as it appeared on the outside. For all his diligence and wisdom, something ate at him deep from within. He was an angry man. He rarely let it show except in acceptable moments of righteous indignation, but in times alone he knew it was there blackening his soul.

His zeal to be the best servant of God in his generation had not led him to the lap of a loving Father, but to the cruel tyranny of his own ego. He had started out with a desire to serve God, but that passion had quickly been consumed by his desire for spiritual status. He loved the looks of admiration and awe that he saw in the eyes of his friends and mentors.

Then one day, on a journey to a distant city he came face to face with the Living God. His encounter was far more dramatic than most. A bright light appeared out of nowhere, knocking him off his horse and blinding his eyes. As he lay there in the dirt, a voice rumbled over his body. "Saul, Saul, why are you persecuting me?"

His next words are quite revealing. "Who are you, Lord?"

He knew he had come face to face with the living God, and now he wasn't sure who he was. But wait! Didn't the voice say Saul had been persecuting him. Surely Saul must have wondered in those brief seconds, "Could this be Jesus?"

What if it was? Saul had killed so many of his followers and was on his way to kill many more. He regarded them as heretics and sought to crush them and their teaching before they could destroy the faith he had embraced since his youth.

Finally the voice spoke again, "I am Jesus, whom you are persecuting."

His worst fears had been realized. The people he had killed in God's name were in fact God's people. What would come of him now? What punishment awaited him in his blind helplessness? Like a man who closes his eyes, cringing in anticipation of being struck by a raised fist, he slowly realizes that no punch is coming. There was no anger, no vengeance.

Saul, later to become Paul the Apostle, had come face to face with the God he had actively warred against, and in that moment all he found was love. The Jesus he had persecuted loved him. He had not come to punish him, but to open his spiritual eyes to see God not as he imagined him to be, but God as he really was.

In that moment, Saul discovered God's favor when had done

absolutely nothing to earn it. Instead of being punished, he received an invitation to come into the family he had tried so hard to destroy. Instead of the death he'd brought to others, he was offered life that he never knew existed.

Saul was left with one inescapable fact. He had done nothing to propel himself above the favor line, but found himself there nonetheless. He found that Jesus had loved him even when he had no idea who he was. For Jesus had shattered the favor line to free Saul from its tyranny. It changed him more than all he'd learned about God previously.

This is where relationship with God begins. It may sound impossible especially if you've hoped for this in the past and, like the young mother who began this chapter, you have only been disappointed by how remote he seemed when you needed him the most. All you knew to do was try even harder to be good enough to win his affection.

But such thinking will never lead you closer to him. Instead of teaching you to love him, it only cements your fear of him even firmer. He wants to break this cycle the only way he can—by making his favor a gift instead of something you could earn.

I have long since lost touch with that mother. If I could speak to her today I'd want her to know that finding favor with God has nothing to do with what we do for him, but what he has already done for us.

Have mercy on me, O God, according to your unfailing love; according to your great compassion blot out my transgressions. Wash away all my iniquity and cleanse me from my sin.

—Psalm 51:1-2

Your personal journey

Are there events in your past that have left you disappointed with God's love for you or overwhelmed you with your own failures? If so, find some time alone with God to go over those moments with him. Ask him to show you how thinking you had to earn his favor might have distorted your perspective of what was really going on. As a regular part of your prayers, ask God to show you where you are trying to earn his favor and ask him to help you see how much he takes delight in you as a loving Father.

What Shall I Give to God?

*"With what shall I come before the Lord and
bow down before the exalted God?...Shall I
offer my firstborn for my transgression,
the fruit of my body for the sin of my soul?"*
—Micah, a prophet (6:6-7)

Sometimes you just can't give things away. At a garage sale my wife and I had before a recent move, I spied a man looking at a reel of electrical wire. We were winding down and I certainly didn't want to throw it away. As he put it down and started to walk away, I told him he could take the wire if he wanted it. He wanted it, but wouldn't take it for free. He walked over to hand me a dollar. I refused. He insisted. We compromised and I gave him fifty cents in change.

We often treat God that way, too. When we realize we cannot earn his love, our fall-back position is to try and compensate him for it. Particularly when we need him to do something for us we will often find ourselves wondering what we can give to him, or give up for him, that will prove our sincerity.

But what is it that we can give to merit his affection? Is tithing enough? What if he wants everything that I own? Could that be enough, after all life is more than possessions? Maybe he wants all of my time too, denying myself any enjoyment or relaxation. Or worse, what if he wants me to go to some far off land and spend the rest of my life spreading the gospel? How many times has that been promised by those on the brink of death, hoping it would convince God to spare them?

But where does that thinking lead? The prophet Micah took it to its obvious end. Aware of his own sinfulness, he begs this exact question: "With what shall I come to God?

"Shall I come before him with burnt offerings, with calves a year old?" It may fit the prescriptions of the law, but is it enough to cleanse Micah's soul? Not exactly.

"Will the Lord be pleased with thousands of rams, with ten thousand rivers of oil?" He has seriously upped the ante here, but he still doesn't think it enough as evidenced in his next offer. "Shall I offer my firstborn for my transgression?" Trading with God will always lead you to the unthinkable as it did for Micah. He wonders if offering his first-born son would be sufficient to atone for his failures and qualify for God's favor. As he so poetically put it, shall I give "the fruit of my body for the sin of my soul?"

In the course of human history it is astounding how many cultures came to that conclusion. When Abraham came into Canaan human sacrifices to Baal, Molech and many other Canaanite deities were the order of the day. Elsewhere throughout the world child sacrifice abounded in tribal rituals to seek the favor of their gods. First-born sons were tied to altars and virgin daughters were offered to fiery volcanoes. Trying to purge our consciousness of guilt by offering a gift we will always end up offering that which is most valuable to us.

But even that cannot be enough. Trying to compensate God for his mercy will lead us to the same futility as trying to earn it and always leave us wondering whether "he loves me, or he loves me not."

"WHY DIDN'T YOU STOP ME?"

We are long past the days of even considering child sacrifice, but that doesn't mean that we don't look for other ways to trade favors with God. Money, time and energy can be used in our attempts to ingratiate God to accept us or work on our behalf. And these in the extreme can destroy us and others around us as surely as worshipping any idol.

No one modeled what it meant to be a committed member of our congregation better than Janice (not her real name). Whenever we needed someone to cook a meal, fill-in for a no-show in our children's ministry or help by spending time with a hurting woman, she was always the first to volunteer. She never said no.

It became so obvious that we actually made announcements that excluded her: "Would anybody but Janice be willing to help out in the nursery today? The person who was supposed to be there called in sick." We all laughed, and then waited for someone else to volunteer.

In return for her service, we showered her with praise. We told her what a gift she was to the body and how special she was to God. We told others, in her hearing, what an example Janice was of every member doing their part in ministry. If we just had a hundred Janice's our congregation would have transformed the city, or so we thought.

There were signs, of course, to all of us that she stretched herself too thin. We knew of struggles in her family and that responsibilities at home went ignored as she was off helping someone else. But frankly, we needed her because others weren't nearly as willing.

One day it came crashing down like a sand castle in the rising surf. What many thought was the enemy trying to destroy her, turned out to be God who was working to set her free. For Janice's serving hadn't entirely come out of her freedom as a loved child of God. Though she had a God-given passion for children, and a heart to serve, somewhere in the process those also became the way for her to earn the acceptance of others, and more importantly of God.

Eventually I left that congregation and found out later that she did as well when I connected with her family some months later. She told me her story. A significant need in her family had caused her to finally give up doing all the ministry others had come to expect of her. Her marriage broke up and she began to ask the difficult questions about her life in God. People who had been blessed by her service, soon distanced themselves from her struggle.

God, however, brought others in her life to help her. He reminded her of simpler times when she had enjoyed the confidence that God loved her and accepted her as his daughter. Somehow all her serving had stolen that simple truth from her. She became like a little girl whose father was too busy for her and had been driven to find a present big enough to catch his attention.

No matter how many of those presents she brought they never seemed to be enough, but for far different reasons than she thought at the time. Fearful that she would never again know Father's love like she had, she allowed the empty place in her heart to be filled by her busy service and the attention from others that it earned her. Rather than encouraging her faithfulness, as we thought we were doing, we were only feeding her insecurity, leading her even further from the relationship with God she desired. That insecurity, along with the needs in her own home, brought her to the brink of personal and emotional bankruptcy.

But the loving Father had never taken his eye off of her. He allowed her to come to the end of her efforts so she could find out just how loved she was. The events had been painful, but they had transformed her. Then she looked at me with tears in her eyes and a voice that wasn't angry, simply pleading for some kind of understanding. "You were my pastor, why didn't you stop me?"

Her words sliced through me as the attention suddenly shifted from her healing, to my complicity in her bondage. She might have driven the car off of the road, but I had helped fill it with gasoline. What could I say? I apologized to her without making any excuses. I had failed her pure and simple.

But the reason I had not stopped her wasn't because I didn't care, it was because I had been on the same course as her, and at the time I hadn't known there was anything wrong with it.

AFTER ALL THIS...

Never the server that Janice was nor facing the same pressures at home, I didn't end up nearly so broken. But, like her, I had a desire to trade my gifts for my Father's affection and like her, I had come to the realization that they were never going to be enough.

My experiences with God began at a very young age. My hunger to know him was piqued by hearing how God involved himself in the lives of ordinary men and women. I also knew at that young age that I was far from sinless and took solace in the God of mercy and forgiveness. I also thought I had to put something forward that would prove to him how serious I was about following him. Looking back, I now know that I was seeking approval from him, by my spiritual passion and willingness to obey him to the best of my ability.

During this time I experienced incredible moments of fellowship with God. I saw him intervene in my life in ways that I knew could only have been him. I heard his voice speak to the depths of my being and guide me in critical decisions I made. I mistakenly thought he was rewarding my offerings to him and continued to lay at his feet whatever I could find that I thought would please him.

But inside, I was never certain that he loved and accepted me—my gifts and sacrifice, perhaps, but not me. The more I gave the more it seemed he wanted, and the best I could do at any moment was to break even with him. I never knew that God was simply delighted with me as his child.

—Not after 35 years of faithfully engaging the spiritual disciplines in varying mixtures and degrees of intensity

—Not after twenty years of professional ministry as a local church pastor.

—Not even after traveling at personal cost and risk to help God's people in third-world countries.

He Loves Me!

At any given moment, I was never sure that God deeply loved me. If you had asked me, I would have told you that he loved me, and for the most part I believed that to be true. After all, Scripture clearly presses that point and I am comfortable talking in such terms. But that still didn't answer my deeper concern. How did he feel about me on any given day?

HE DELIGHTS IN YOU

The words of the Old Testament prophet seemed only a distant dream, "He will take great delight in you, he will quiet you with his love, he will rejoice over you with singing." Except for fleeting moments, few and far between, I couldn't imagine that this is the way God felt about me. How could he with the temptations that I battled?

I don't think it takes any of us long who probe such questions honestly to see enough failures and wasted time that would give God ample justification to set us aside and to ignore the requests we make of him.

Jesus warned us that there would be people who would prophesy, cast out demons and work many miracles in his name, who he would turn away at the judgment. "I never knew you. Depart from me." If that isn't a great example of climbing the ladder that's leaning on the wrong wall, I don't know what is. I didn't want to be caught with that crowd.

These moments of insecurity would drive me to my knees in repentance, and make me redouble my efforts to be more committed to God. Though I could sustain the increased burden for a few weeks or months, I never had any certainty that the things I was doing were enough to cause him to be delighted with me. Eventually, I would slide back to where I had been before.

I'll never forget when all of that changed. A few years ago, through a painful betrayal and a fresh insight into God's work for us on the cross, I began to see how much my Father loved me and to understand how much delight he took in his children. It has radically changed my life and it is my hope that the telling of it in the pages ahead will help transform yours as well.

God doesn't need us to serve him as a means to attain his

love or affection. He wants us serving him out of the love and affection he already holds in his heart for us. If you have never tasted that reality, you cannot imagine the freedom that is yours. My Father brought me to the place where I realized that even if I never preached another sermon, never counseled another person nor ever led someone to Christ again, he still delighted in me as his child.

That doesn't mean he approves of everything I do, but it has freed me to know that he loves me—absolutely and completely. I had served God for 34 years always with an undercurrent of trying to earn his favor. It has only been in the last four that I've learned to live in that favor and I'm never going back.

That's when it became clear. It is not the fear of losing God's favor that takes us to the depth of fellowship with him and transforms our lives with his holiness. It is our certainty of knowing that favor, even in the midst of our weakness and failure, that lead us to the fullness of his life.

Fearing had never taken me to the depths of his life or his transforming power; discovering his delight has. I now know that the key to God's favor doesn't rest on what I could give him, but what he already had given to me.

He delights in you, too. Can you see him that way over you, exalting and dancing with joy?

No? Do you think your failures and doubts diminish his love for you? Are you afraid you can't bring enough to make him notice?

Then come with me and let me show you something. He doesn't delight in you because of your deeds or your gifts. He delights in you simply because you are his.

The Lord your God is with you...he will take great delight in you, he will quiet you with his love, he will rejoice over you with singing.
—ZEPHANIAH 3:17

For your personal journey

Take an honest look at the spiritual things you give your life to. Are they rising out of your security of God's great love for you or an attempt to earn his affection? Do you live trying to pay God back for his salvation, or some other act of his on your behalf? Ask God to begin to rearrange your thinking and to help you understand that his love goes far beyond any gift you can bring him.

The Businessman and the Beggar

> *When we accept ownership of our powerlessness*
> *and helplessness, when we acknowledge that we*
> *are paupers at the door of God's mercy, then God*
> *can make something beautiful out of us.*
> **BRENNAN MANNING IN *THE RAGAMUFFIN GOSPEL***

It turned out to be a tale of two men. These are the only two encounters Mark thought significant to record from Jesus' last trip to Jerusalem and his impending death. One was at the beginning of the journey, near his home base of Galilee. The other came on the trip's last leg, in the city of Jericho before he would ascend to Jerusalem.

Two men, each in dire need, approached Jesus for help. Clearly, Jesus extends his favor to both of them, but as we shall see only one received it. The other went away from his moment with Jesus, his countenance shattered, grieved because he had misunderstood the offer Jesus made to him.

Watch each of them carefully. Why does one receive and the other does not? If you're like me, you'll see yourself in both of them at various times in your life. But now you'll know which example will show you how you respond to God, and which will take your best intentions and turn them against you.

The answer may surprise you because it is the opposite of everything most of us have been trained to think about God and how he works in us.

CAUGHT IN THE DOING

Jesus had no more begun his journey to Jerusalem, when a man ran up to him, stopped him and knelt before him in the dirt. "Good Teacher, what must I do to inherit eternal life?" Both his pace and his posture testify to the desperation in his request. He knew Jesus had something he lacked and wanted to find out his secret before he left town.

The question certainly sounds genuine enough, even humble. Jesus answers by referring him to the commandments.

The businessman's answer tells us a lot about him. "I have kept all of these from my youth up."

Really? Of course we know now and Jesus knew at the time that this answer wasn't possible. Paul told us that no one has ever kept all of God's law and that if even one person could have earned eternal life by the law, then Christ would have died in vain. If this man had been genuine, he would have known that. The Father had only given the law so that we might come to the end of ourselves and know that we needed someone to rescue us. Any genuine pursuit of the law would have led this man to the same conclusion.

Does that mean he was lying? Not necessarily. Though he had not kept the law, what was most critical in this exchange was that he genuinely thought he had. Since he was a little child he had worked hard to keep the law, in hopes of earning his place in God's kingdom.

For him to think he had kept the law, however, he had to recreate it in his own image. In other words he would have created loopholes in his mind to justify those portions he had not kept, perhaps only focusing on major parts of the law such as murder and adultery and excusing his own hate, lust, or selfishness.

By his own desperation we know he had missed the point. The fact that he was still seeking eternal life made it clear that he hadn't found it yet, nor was he confident that his current course would produce it. He wanted something more to do.

This man was steeped in his own works. That was evident by the question he had asked at the outset. The "I" and the "do" gave him away—"What must I do...?" He was focused on himself, his ability and resources; trying so hard to earn what Jesus wanted to give him.

How Jesus wanted him to understand that! Mark specifically mentions that Jesus looked on him with deep affection. What did he see? Did he see a little boy trying to be perfect as the only way to earn his father's affirmation? Did he see the years of fruitless labor this man had endured? Could he see the twisted motives he used to justify himself and maintain his illusion of righteousness? Did he see the gnawing in the young man's stomach, born of his obsessive drive to perfection that was destroying him from within?

Probably he saw all that and more, and Jesus wanted him to see it too. His next response seems on the surface to be one of Jesus' most insensitive comments: "One thing you lack: go and sell all you possess, and give it to the poor, and you shall have treasure in heaven; and come, follow Me." On hearing the words, the businessman's countenance fell. Unable to do that, he walked away in grief.

How often I've taught this parable, and with unwitting arrogance, railed at the rich man's inability to do what Jesus asked of him. He was too greedy to follow Jesus, I had said. He loved his money more than God and now he would pay for it.

But, honestly, was that the point? Who would have come to this kingdom if those were the terms? When I first went forward at a Billy Graham crusade all I was asked to do was repent and believe in him. If he'd asked me to sell everything I owned and give it to the poor, I doubt I would have gone forward. I doubt anyone else would have either. In fact I've never met one person who ever came to Christ on those terms nor many who would stay if he required it of them today!

To condemn the man for not doing so is not only arrogant of us, but misses Jesus' point entirely. He was not offering the man the opportunity to buy his salvation. He only wanted him to discover what his attempts to keep the law already should have—that he didn't have enough in himself to meet any standard of qualification for God's life.

RAISING THE BAR

Coaches don't train young high jumpers by putting the bar at world-record height and challenging them to try and jump it. They put it at a height their charges can successfully achieve and then, over the course of time, slowly raise the bar allowing refined technique, practice and conditioning to help them jump higher.

But Jesus doesn't do that here. Responding to the rich man's request, Jesus puts the bar forty feet in the air. Jump that! And the rich businessman did exactly what any athlete would do, he went away discouraged, knowing the task was impossible.

The man understood the lesson, but missed the point. Jesus wasn't trying to be mean to him. He raised the bar beyond the man's ability to get over it precisely because Jesus wanted him to stop trying. The gift he offered the man was to be free of the incredible burden of having to earn God's love by his own efforts. He was caught in his own doing and Jesus was trying to free him.

He was hoping the young man would look him in the eye and say, "I can't do that!" To which Jesus might have answered, "Good, then stop doing all the other silly things you're trying to do to earn God's favor. Stop striving, stop pretending, stop trying to earn that which you can never earn!"

Jesus didn't want him living any longer under the tyranny of the favor line, but he knew how difficult it is for people of great resource to find their way into his kingdom. Such people always feel like they can earn it or pay for it. They are too focused on their own efforts and resources to simply receive God's gift.

His dependence on his own resources was robbing them of the life he sought. No matter how much he could do, such efforts would never cover the empty place in their heart that seeks God's approval. For it's only in that realization that we can discover what it really means to be approved as God's child and find security in his love for us.

That's not to say that as we love him he won't bring us greater freedom from our possessions and show us the joy of generosity, for he will. But that will rise not out of our attempts to earn his favor, but as grateful responses to the favor he already offers us.

Even when Peter started to boast that he and the others had left everything to follow him, Jesus reminds him that none of them had left anything that he wasn't replacing with far more and far better. The fact is they had left their stuff not to earn eternal life, but because of a relationship with Jesus that had captured their hearts.

Sadly, we don't get to see the end for this young businessman. My hope is that Jesus' words finally worked through his heart. But whether they did or didn't, Jesus still offered him an incredible gift—the secret to God's favor.

"LORD, HAVE MERCY!"

As Jesus was departing Jericho a few days later for his final walk up the barren heights to the city of Jerusalem, another man wanted his help. This man was a blind beggar sitting by the side of the road. He heard a great commotion around him, he wanted to know what it was. Someone told him that Jesus of Nazareth was passing through on his way to Jerusalem for the feast.

Bartimaeus had already heard enough about this teacher from Galilee to know that he the power to help him. He began to cry out, "Jesus, Son of David, have mercy on me!"

People nearby were embarrassed by his shouts and sternly told him to keep quiet. He was only a beggar after all, why would Jesus care about him? But that only made Bartimaeus cry even louder and above all the other noise Jesus heard him. He had Bartimaeus brought to him and he made his request. "I want to regain my sight."

Notice that he did not ask what he needed to do to see again. He did not barter based on any qualification he might have to make him worthy. He simply put all of his confidence in the mercy of the man from God.

And that was enough.

Jesus didn't ask him to sell all he had. Jesus healed him and noted that Bartimaeus' simple focus was all that was needed. "Go, your way; your faith has saved you." Not only did he receive healing, but salvation as well.

Jesus did not love the beggar more than the businessman, nor did he give to one and not the other. For he graciously gave to both of them. It's just that one recognized it and one did not and the difference between the two contains all we need to know to find life in God.

Jesus didn't want the disciples to miss that point. Even before he had left on this journey he had told them a parable that these encounters had illustrated perfectly. He told of a Pharisee and a tax collector entering the temple. The Pharisee delighted in his righteousness—how he was more committed than anyone else he knew. He even puffed himself up at the expense of the tax collector praying nearby, "God, I thank you that I am not like other people... even like this tax collector."

That's what living by our own works produces. Since we'll never be good enough on our own we will seek to justify ourselves by being better than most other believers around us. To create that façade we have to focus on their weaknesses and hold them in contempt. Any time we set ourselves above others, we only demonstrate how little we understand God's mercy.

The tax-collector on the other hand was not even willing to look up to heaven, but beat his chest praying, "God, be merciful to me, the sinner!" Then Jesus asked which one went home justified? The answer was obvious, as obvious as Jesus' encounter with the businessman and the beggar.

When you are tempted to stake your relationship with God on your own goodness or your sacrifice, don't even try. Picture the bar so high that you'll never find a way to clear it. Approach God on the basis of your own efforts and you will always go away disappointed and disillusioned. But that is not bad news.

What it means is that God has fulfilled in himself everything he would ever require of us. Abandoning our own attempts to establish our own worthiness is central to the power of the gospel. Learn that and a door stands before you that will lead you to the very heart of a loving Father. This is the way to know that he delights over you with joy, and is able to transform you into the fullness of his glory.

He absolutely, completely loves you. Discovering how much will revolutionize your relationship to him and your life in this world.

> But go and learn what this means: "I desire mercy, not sacrifice." For I have not come to call the righteous, but sinners.
>
> —MATTHEW 9:13

ॐ   ॐ   ॐ

For your personal journey

Spend some time with God considering your own relationship to him. Do your requests of God look more like the businessman or the beggar? Do you begin every day aware of your performance or willing to stake it on God's mercy? We've all been taught that life in God is something we earn with diligent effort and this isn't easy to unlearn. Ask him to help you understand his mercy and how you can stop trying to jump over a bar you will never reach.

The God We Love to Fear

The Christian ideal has not been tried and found wanting.
It has been found difficult and left untried.

G.K. CHESTERTON

It was a strange game we played as little children. We used to scare ourselves half to death just for the sheer joy of it.

We would be sitting around the front yard of someone's home, when suddenly one of us would point down the street saying we saw a kidnapper sneaking up towards us. The rest of us would mockingly feign to be afraid.

"I'm not kidding," he would say, "I know I saw him looking this way." For a while he would continue the ploy and we would not believe him. Eventually someone else would join the story and point out something he thought looked suspicious, a glance our direction by someone walking up the street, or a car passing by too slowly. Then the game was on.

Everyone contributed to the story in hopes of scaring the

others off the porch. The last one to run was the winner. But we were young and it usually didn't take long. At some point in the process reality would get distorted and we'd all believe our own stories. Suddenly we'd burst off the porch, running for the backyard and down into the safety of the basement.

After a while our fears would subside and we would, laughing, retell how scared we got. Then we'd go out front to see if we could spot anymore kidnappers. The whole process would repeat itself until we again ran to the basement for safety.

It was only a game, but it allowed us to taste the power of fear. Even when we were making it up ourselves and dared to resist it, it could still win over us.

A POWERFUL FORCE

If you've ever tried to go to sleep at night with fear preying on your mind, you also know its incredible power. Even when we can rationally discount it, fear nevertheless forces its will upon us, like a relentless rising tide.

Those who motivate people know that nothing works better. I see it in my work helping public schools navigate the treacherous waters where church and state issues collide. All of the letters sent out by advocacy groups on the right and the left appeal exclusively to fear of what the other side is doing to destroy "the America we all hold dear." They know nothing works better to make people send in their money or volunteer their time and energy.

Fear permeates life in this age. It's what makes you go to work in the morning. lock your doors at night and makes your heart race when a policeman pulls in behind you. Advertisers use it and so do friends and family when they want you to do what they think is best.

> And there is so much to fear—
> We fear the unknown.
> We fear being unknown.
> We fear not having enough.
> We fear getting caught.

We fear we'll never find the right person to marry.
We fear debilitating or life-threatening diseases.
We fear for our children's safety.
We fear what other people think of us.
We fear they won't.
We fear crime.
We fear losing a loved one.
We fear authority.
We fear that we won't get the things we desire most.
We fear what others might do to us.
We fear rejection.
We fear failure.
We fear being taken advantage of.
We fear being alone.
We fear losing our job.
We fear people finding out we're not all we claim to be.
We fear something bad might happen to us.
We fear not fitting in.
We fear death.

No wonder it's not easy to sleep some nights and no wonder we are bombarded with the symptoms of stress, all the way from headaches to depression. Fear is so powerful that almost all of our human institutions use various forms of it to keep people under control. Offering the right combination of rewards and punishments they can easily exploit people's fears to make them do what they otherwise wouldn't choose to do.

It would be easier to make the point here if fear always led us to do harmful and destructive things, but that simply isn't true. Sometimes fear will lead us to prudent decisions. The fear of getting caught might win over our temptation to do something wrong. The fear of losing our job will induce us to work harder than we would otherwise.

In a fallen world, fear is the only way to hold society in check. Caring for nothing more than our own self-interest, the fear of hurtful consequences is the foundation of all laws and authority. Before Jesus died on the cross, there was nothing else. Even God used fear to help keep sin in check among his people. "The fear of the Lord is the beginning of wisdom," wrote the Psalmist. We come to the regrettable conclusion that fear isn't our problem—only what we fear. If we can fear the awesome, holy God more than anything else in our lives it will lead us to the right path, or so we think.

Thus we come to view fear in ambivalent terms. Fear of what others might think can lead us down a wrong path, but fearing God can help motivate us to holiness. We think it's not *what* we fear that matters, but *who* we fear.

WON BY FEAR

Just look at the history of Christianity. Teaching people to fear God and his judgments have been used more than any other motive to hold the faithful in check. It is readily accepted now as the best way to get people to follow God.

Saint Cecile Cathedral sits high above every other building in the village of Albi, located in the southern region of France. Like the Sistine Chapel in the Vatican, the ceiling and walls of the magnificent edifice are painted with Biblical scenes.

The entire story of the Bible has been painted across the ceiling over a brilliant blue background. Beginning at the back of the cathedral with creation and Eden and finishing in front with the Last Judgment. There, behind the altar and overwhelming it by its sheer size is one of the largest full-color pictorial compositions in the world, nearly forty feet tall and thirty feet wide. In its original form, the painting depicted God enthroned at the center, judging between the sheep and the goats.

The latter are cast into the torment of hell, agonizingly represented in seven individual panels that take up the entire bottom of the composition. Each are fifteen feet in height and show how those guilty of each of the seven mortal sins will be tormented in hell. For instance, the greedy are shown bound, with demons pouring molten gold down their throats.

Constructed in the fourteenth century this scene depicts what the designers firmly wanted in the minds of the faithful as they gathered in the Cathedral. God is a terrible judge, and terrible things will happen to those who do not do what he says. It's a refrain often heard in Christian history—even to the present.

Waiting to get into a Celine Dion concert recently with my wife, we were confronted with a gaggle of signs announcing our eminent consignment to hell. "Don't you care that you are headed for hell?" someone shouted in my face from only a few steps away. "Repent, or you will burn in agony forever!" someone else called out across the crowd.

I've no doubt these people were well-intentioned, seeing this as the best way to lead people to God. It was obvious, however, that the crowd around them was not convinced. Most ignored them resenting the imposition of their message on a captive audience.

Through most of its history, Christianity has been insepa-rable from the God of judgment. The panels in the Cathedral at Alibi, Jonathan Edwards' *Sinners In the Hands of an Angry God*, or the invitation to receive Christ, "because you could die tonight and go to hell," all seek to build on this foundation of fear. While it is effective to prompt people to make on-the-spot commitments to Christ, it has rarely led to spiritual passion and growth.

Isn't it odd that the most compelling argument to know God is the horror of not doing so? I find no such preoccupation in the ministry of Jesus for those who followed him. Certainly he and writers of the New Testament warned us about the destruc-tiveness of sin and the consequences that befall those who neglect his offer of salvation. But he did not use that fear to induce people to follow him.

His invitation was to a God who loved them completely and to a kingdom more valuable than anything they had ever known. He didn't use their fears because he knew that fear was part of the problem, even their fear of God. Though it might be easily manipulated to secure a temporal response, it would never be enough to bring them to the fullness of his Father's glory.

WHEN FEAR IS NOT ENOUGH

I thought I'd missed the rapture, and for a twelve-year-old boy, that can be pretty unnerving.

Through a tragic comedy of errors at my junior high school, I had not received a message my parents had sent telling me not to get on the bus after school. They would be picking me up.

So I boarded the bus as usual. Only this day was different. To start with, my older brothers who always boarded first at the high school weren't there. A few minutes later when we arrived at the grammar school on the route, my youngest brother wasn't in line there either. How could this be, I wondered?

Immediately I remembered the words the pastor had spoken the Sunday before at church. Talking about the Second Coming of Christ, he told about two people in a field. One was taken, the other left to face the torment of the Great Tribulation. "If there is one unconfessed sin between you and God when Jesus comes again, you'll be left." It didn't take me long sitting on that bus without the rest of my family to come up with a whole list of things that could have kept me out of the rapture.

That bus ride home was the longest of my life. By the time I'd gotten to my stop, my imagination had run wild. I was certain now that I had missed the rapture. I ran up our quarter-mile long driveway, hoping against hope that at least one of my parents would still be home. But they weren't.

I was devastated. I prayed. I cried. I repented. I begged God to take me even if a bit late, but all to no avail. Terrified of the tribulation to come, I knew that going to hell would be even worse. I then and there determined that I would be faithful to God no matter what the Antichrist tried to do to me. Even though I'd blown the first chance, I would not the second. In the arrogance of youth, I prepared myself to face the Antichrist.

An hour later my parents returned with the rest of the family and the miscommunication unraveled. I hadn't missed the rapture after all! I was elated with the news, but I was taking no chances on the future. I was going to be the best twelve-year-old God ever had.

For the next month, I probably was. As best I knew, I lived

sinlessly, avoiding any temptation that surfaced and spending time in prayer and Bible reading every day. But it didn't last. As the days passed, so did the reality of my fear until some months later I had ended up right back where I had begun.

Jesus knew that fear, like a crutch for someone with a broken leg, is only a temporary fix. Though it can be a heady motivation in the short-term, it is absolutely worthless for the long-haul. As such it doesn't really change us, it only controls us as long as our fear can be stoked. That's why sermons on God's judgment are so common in Christianity. They confront us with our fears of God and seek to provoke us to live the way we know we should. The repentance that follows and the resolve to rededicate ourselves to Christ's purpose, makes us feel clean again.

Such experience actually help us live better for awhile—but only for awhile. Eventually the passion of such moments fade and the old self encroaches its way back into our lives. We end up caught in the same patterns from which we had repented. Soon the cycle repeats itself.

Fear cannot lead us to life-long transformation, but only a momentary reformation of behavior. Instead of inviting us to enter into relationship with the Living God, it pushes us away with feelings of inadequacy and repetitious failure.

Jesus had a far better way. He wanted to break the bondage of fear itself—even our fear of God. He knew of a force far more powerful—one that would not fade with the passing of time and would invite us into the depths of relationship with God. He would settle for nothing else. Why should we?

> Do not be afraid, little flock, for your Father has been pleased to give you the kingdom.
> —LUKE 12:32

☙   ☙   ☙

For your personal journey

Think back to the time you first made a commitment to Christ. Did it come because you were overwhelmed with his love, or because you were afraid of his punishment? When you think now of God watching you every moment of every day, do you find that comforting or scary? Do you see fearing him as a necessary motive to help you avoid sin and do the things you think God wants you to do and if so, has it helped you avoid all the sins in your life? Think through these questions as you ask God to show you how your fear of him might be keeping you from feeling safe in his presence.

The Most Powerful Force in the Universe

*Won't the awareness that God loves us
no matter what lead to spiritual laziness and
moral laxity? Theoretically, this seems a
reasonable fear, but in reality the opposite is true...
The more rooted we are in the love of God,
the more generously we will live our faith.*
BRENDAN MANNING IN *LION AND LAMB*

"Do you love me?" Is there a harder question you can be asked by someone you care about? It implies that you've done something to suggest otherwise. How do you answer with words when your actions fall so far short?

"Do you love me?"

The words must have sliced to the depths of Peter's heart as Jesus probed him. It had been a little over a week since Peter had abandoned Jesus at his greatest moment of need. After promising he would die for Jesus, Peter's fears had caught up to him. In the heat of the moment he had proved to all that he had loved his own life more than he had loved his friend.

Jesus had already asked the question twice, referring to the greatest depth of love any person could offer another. Both times, Peter could not say that he did. In the verbal dance they engaged in that morning on the shore of Galilee, Peter had answered with a different word for love than Jesus had used. "I have great affection for you, as a brother," he responded.

We are not told why he couldn't answer with the word that Jesus used, but it is easy to assume his failure might well have played into it. Peter knew he had not loved him as much as he thought, and perhaps in the face of his denial tried to find a word that would more honestly fit his actions.

When he asks him the third time, Jesus switches to Peter's word for brotherly affection. Though Peter answers in the affirmative he is hurt by the fact that he'd been asked three times. But notice how undeterred Jesus is by his answers. All three times he invites Peter past his weakness to ministry in his kingdom. "Take care of my sheep." His message is clear. You're not damaged goods. Your failure has not changed anything between us. You're still in the family.

This exchange is fascinating for a number of reasons, but perhaps the most incredible is not the answer he seeks of Peter, but the simple fact that Jesus asked the question at all.

What God ever cares about being loved?

THE GOD WHO WANTS TO BE LOVED

"Do you love me?"

It's not exactly a question we expect God to ask, and yet John records it as one of the significant conversations the resurrected Jesus had with one of his disciples. That he asks it more than once focuses even more attention to it.

Why would he care about being loved? He is Almighty God enthroned in the presence of thousands of adoring angels. He can command obedience simply because he is the greatest power in the universe. Why would he be seeking Peter's love?

We seem to be far more comfortable when our deities command fear. Almost every idol or false god man has ever created seeks the submission of his or her subjects by sheer terror. But love? What false god ever wanted to be loved? Feared? Yes! Obeyed? Yes. But never loved.

After his work on the cross was finished, however, Jesus comes looking for love, and he seeks it from the one who had just failed him most. Could this be what he most wanted the cross to produce in his followers? Was his death designed to reach past their fears of God and begin a new relationship with them based on the intimacy of love instead? What else could it be?

Throughout the Old Testament God often identified himself as the God of love and mercy, but few understood him that way. They seemed only able to obey him under threat or judgment. Even commanding them to love him with all their hearts, seemed to negate the end by the means employed. Can true love really be commanded?

What Jesus seeks from Peter reflects what the Father had always wanted from his people, but what they have rarely understood. He desires the warmth and tenderness of a relationship filled with love. None of this was lost on Peter, even though his answer didn't come easily. If the power of the cross can reach past that failure, then something new had really happened. Jesus was inviting Peter past his failure to experience the depths of God's love—to tap into the most powerful force in the universe.

Love lies at the very core of God's nature. In fact, when John sums up the substance of God he does so in a very simple statement: "God is love." We may not be able to explain in concrete terms all that God is and how Father, Son and Spirit relate together in such unity, but we do know that they exist in a perfect state of love.

When that love touches you, you will discover there is nothing more powerful in the entire universe. It is more powerful than your failures, your sins, your disappointments, your dreams and even your fears. God knew that when you tap the depths of his love, your life would forever be changed. Nothing can prevail over it; and nothing else will lead you to taste of his kind of holiness.

STRONGER THAN FEAR

I am not saying in this that the fear of God is wrong, only that it is incomplete. It is the first rung on the ladder to knowing God in his fullness. He said himself it was the beginning of wisdom, but it is only the beginning. Love is the end of it.

If you don't love God, you would be well-served to fear him. At least that might keep you from destructive behaviors that will destroy you and others around you. But once you know how much he loves you, you'll never need to fear him again. In other words, this Father doesn't just seek our obedience, he seeks our love. He can have your obedience without your love, but he knows where he has your love he will also have your obedience.

"There is no fear in love, because fear has to do with punishment," John wrote as he tried to convince the church in Ephesus that God's love had replaced the old order of fear. It was revolutionary then, and regrettably still is today. We seem more comfortable fearing God than we do loving him.

But fear isn't in God's nature. He fears nothing. Thus his own holiness is not produced by his fear, but by his love. In fact, fear cannot produce the holiness God wants to share with us. It is incapable of doing so. For God to transform us to be like him, he must expel our fear and teach us the wonder of living in his love.

John paints fear and love as polar opposites. Before the coming of Jesus, God used fear to hold our passions in check, but it never made anyone holy. In Christ, God appealed to us on the basis of love. Thus he needs our fear no longer, knowing we will never love that which we fear.

You might honestly believe the highway patrol officer behind you in traffic is looking out for your safety, but that doesn't endear you to him. In fact, the fear of getting a ticket will make you extra careful about every move you make. For the time he is near you in traffic, you are safer than any other time on the road. Not only are you driving more safely, but so are the other drivers around you.

But does that keep you from being relieved when he finally turns to go another direction? Even though his presence was more helpful to you than you might realize, it didn't make you want to become his friend. The motives of conformity do not produce intimacy.

This is where organized religion so often gets it backwards and why so many people in the pews remain so distant from God and so unchanged in their character. We think conformity to God's ways will lead us closer to him, when the opposite is true. Our intimate relationship with him is what will transform us.

Fearing God can compel us to conform our behavior to his desires, but it will not last. Because it convinces us to act against our will, even when it leads us to righteousness, it does not change us. The behavior that results only lasts as long as the fear itself, which is why those who approach it this way will need greater levels of fear to stay motivated.

He knows that responding to his love will take you much further than fear ever could. That's why love must first deal with your fears. "Perfect love drives out fear," John continues. While fear may be the most powerful motive known to man, God's love is more powerful still and in the face of it our greatest fears are swallowed up in him. Love displaces fear the same way light displaces darkness.

There is nothing more critical to spiritual growth than making this transition. John concludes, "The one who fears is not made perfect in love" (1 John 4:18). As long as we live in fear, we exclude ourselves from the very process that will make us complete in God.

People who serve God because they fear his punishment will forever try to please him by doing the best that they can and will find they will always come up short. Dominated by guilt and having to justify themselves in failure, they never discover what it really means to become God's friend.

God has better things in mind for you. He wants you to know his love so completely that fearing him will have no place. When you are absolutely convinced how much God loves you, it will drive out every fear you have. You won't need to fear an uncertain future, the rejection of friends, the lack of desires, or even God himself. Knowing his heart for you will free you to trust him more than ever and that alone will lead you to ever-greater participation in his holiness.

WHAT MANNER OF LOVE

You would think being free from the fear of the Lord would be great news, but I don't find that everyone shares my excitement. Many see their fear of God, or eternal judgment, as the only thing that keeps them from indulging in sin. Without it, they are so afraid they would give into their flesh, that they cling to their fear of God as if it was a life raft in a frothing sea.

It is difficult to give up your fear of God if it has served you so well. That's understandable. We don't often think of love as a compelling enough motive to hold us in check. We all know that we loved our parents, but not enough to keep us from doing things they told us not to do. Only the fear of getting caught and punished was enough to deter us from wrongdoing. Many of us transfer that same idea to God so it is no wonder we trust our fear more than his love.

But the love God extends to us and invites from us is nothing like any love we have known before. "This is how we know what love is: Jesus Christ laid down his life for us" (1 John 3:16). John defines our Father's love for us because he knew that our earthly references to love would never do justice to God's.

Love in earthly terms is invariably tied to self-interest. That's why people talk about falling in love, or out of love. What they mean is that they feel affection for someone when they bring some benefit to them. However, when they no longer provide benefit, or become more of a burden than a joy, we don't feel the same way about them. Haven't we all had what we thought were close friends, who turned on us the minute we no longer served their interests? Haven't we done the same to others? Self-centered "love" can only seek its own good.

Only in the rarest moments will someone's love for another call them to deny their self-interest and sacrifice themselves for another. Probably the greatest stories in literature play to this theme and are the ones that touch us so deeply. They provide a glimpse into the eternal. Rare indeed are the relationships in this world that rise to such self-sacrifice.

But that's exactly what Jesus did for you. By doing so he turned the definition of love upside down. God's love is not based on *selfishness*, but *selflessness*. He didn't give his life on the cross to serve himself, but to serve us who were lost in our sins. By doing so he modeled a love for us that we can only find in him. This love gives up its own desires in the face of greater good. It is not meant to be the subject of fiction, but the way we live every day.

That may seem incredibly remote from your life. We're not wired to think in such terms, having learned from a very young age that if you're going to survive in this world you have to look out for yourself. We have no idea how to love selflessly and no ability to conjure it up out of our own commitment or devotion.

John said it best. "We love because he first loved us" (1 John 4:19). Until we experience the full depth of God's love, and are able to trust him with every detail of our lives, we will not break free from the power of self. That's why it is so critical to understand Jesus' death on the cross as an act of love for you. This teaching has been too long neglected among God's people. If you see it only as God satisfying his justice, then you unwittingly empty the cross of its power.

The doorway into the Father's love begins at the cross. Seeing what Father and Son accomplished together in that climactic moment defines love in a way that you can only experience in him. This is the love that will allow you to feel perfectly safe in the Father's presence. It frees you to be exactly who you are, weaknesses and all, and never again have to pretend before him.

Then you will discover that life in God rises out of your security in his love, not your insecurity that you don't love him enough. That's the lesson Jesus wanted to teach Peter that morning by Galilee's shore. Though Peter could not answer that he loved Jesus to the depth that Jesus asked, he had more to learn of the cross' power. He had a fear of his own failures that had not been swallowed up by God's love.

This was a transforming moment for Peter, and though, he couldn't get it right here, he eventually did. When he wrote his letters, the only love he speaks of towards God was the depth of love with which Jesus had addressed him. He finally tapped into a love so deep that he never needed fear again.

So can you.

Let's go to Golgotha and watch the most incredible plan ever devised unfold in all its glory.

> *For you did not receive a spirit that makes you a slave again to fear, but you received the Spirit of sonship. And by him we cry, "Abba, Father."*
> —ROMANS 8:15

For your personal journey

Are most of your actions about God, motivated by your security in his love for you, or your fear that if you don't do enough, God might not be pleased with you? Ask him to show you the ways your fears motivate you in day-to-day decisions. Read through 1 John 4:7-21 every morning for a few days and mediate on John's words there. Ask him to help you discover how much he loves you and in doing so to drive out the fears in your life.

The Undeniable Proof

*If God is for us, who can be against us? He who
did not spare his own Son, but gave him up for us
all—how will he not also, along with him,
graciously give us all things?*

—Romans 8:31–32

He Loved You Enough to Let You Go

By giving humans freedom of will, the Creator has chosen to limit his own power. He risked the daring experiment of giving us the freedom to make good or bad decisions, to live decent or evil lives, because God does not want the forced obedience of slaves. Instead, he covets the voluntary love and obedience of sons who love him for himself.
CATHERINE MARSHALL, *BEYOND OUR SELVES*

"It was about obedience, pure and simple." The words drifted over from an animated conversation two tables away in the restaurant where I was having lunch. "That's all God wanted from Adam and Eve and they couldn't give it." The rest nodded in approval.

How I wanted to interrupt my conversation and join theirs. I used to think that too. All that matters to God is our obedience. Weren't we all taught that?

I've since come to discover it isn't so. Certainly God wants us to be obedient to him, and Adam and Eve would have saved us all a host of grief if they had obeyed him. But God knew their disobedience was only a symptom of something he cared about far more.

Since he created us so that we could share in the relationship that Father, Son and Spirit have shared for all eternity, then we have to engage it the same way they do. Their unity flows from the fact that they absolutely love and trust each other. You can see it in the way they talk to each other and how they act together. It only makes sense that God's invitation for us to share in that relationship must be based on that same trust.

One can obey God, and yet not trust him, and in doing so miss out on a relationship with him. One cannot, however, trust God and be disobedient to him. For we shall see that all disobedience flows out of mistrust in God's nature and of his intentions toward us.

Thus the experience in the Garden wasn't to demand their obedience but to incubate their trust. He knew that the first step might well be a step away from him in disobedience. He knew the lesson would be painful and costly—for him most of all—but he chose it because he desired people who would relate to him in love, not obey him in fear. It would have been far easier to accomplish the latter, but God knew that love could only flourish where trust does; and that real trust could only emerge where people were free to reject it.

As bizarre as the actions of the father of the prodigal son might seem to us, it made perfect sense to Jesus. He had already seen it happen a long time before in a garden called Eden. For his Father had provided everything Adam and Eve could have ever wanted, even the freedom to live apart from him.

By doing so, he gave them the greatest of all possible gifts— the potential to enter into a free and loving relationship with the God of the universe. That they chose first to trust their own wisdom and plunge the creation into the agony of sin was less his concern than how he would use that failure to invite them back to himself.

I'D RATHER DO IT MYSELF

God filled Eden with luscious fruit trees of every variety, but in the middle of it planted two special trees. The Tree of Life would impart immortality to any who ate of it. The Tree of Knowledge would open their eyes to see good and evil like God sees it. He told them they were free to eat from every tree except the Tree of Knowledge. Though its fruit would enlighten, it would also kill them.

Wouldn't it have been better if he had never created it, or at least hid it in some distant corner of the globe? Certainly its presence provided the opportunity for mankind's greatest failure and with it thousands of years of suffering in sin, pain, conflict and disease. But God didn't plant that tree to spell our demise; but to allow us the freedom that would make relationship with him meaningful.

He knew that whichever way Adam and Eve chose, it would still be the first step on a journey to learn how to trust his awesome love. Regrettably, like the prodigal son, however, they would only learn to trust God by first trusting themselves and finding out just how misguided that is.

"You could be like God," the serpent promised them that morning as he enticed them to eat what God had forbidden. What a devastating temptation! One could want worse things than to be like God. Didn't God already make them in his image? Wasn't his desire to invite them into a relationship with him that would make them like him? Isn't the desire to be like God the highest ideal of the Christian life?

That such a noble motive could be used for such evil, should be a warning to us. For here sin is clearly unmasked. We often view sin as evil actions alone and miss the nature of sin itself. At its root, sin is simply grabbing for ourselves what God has not given to us. In this realm, our best intentions can draw us into as much bondage as our most indulgent desires.

Adam and Eve's sin was not *what* they wanted, but *how* they went about getting it. Would they trust God to make them like him, or would they reach out and take it for themselves?

Is that what Jesus understood when he rejected Satan's

enticement to change stones into bread after his long fast? There was certainly nothing evil in the act itself. Nothing in Moses' law forbade it and it wouldn't have been any different than changing water into wine, which he would do a few days later. Jesus, however, trusted his Father to bring to him everything he needed. Fulfilling his own ambitions, wholesome though they may be, would take him down the same path as Adam and Eve.

He knew God's gifts are always two-edged. They can be used for his glory, or abused for our ambitions. Jesus chose the former; Adam and Eve the latter. The tree that stood before them in the Garden was no symbol or loyalty test. Its fruit held real spiritual power. Those who would eat of it would see good and evil the same way God sees it; and that is exactly what happened to Adam and Eve. As soon as their teeth plunged into its fruit their eyes were opened to see good and evil; and the first thing they noticed was how evil they had become. That knowledge overwhelmed them with shame and shattered their relationship with God.

A LIE EXPERTLY PLACED

All it took for the enemy to wreak such havoc in God's innocent creation was to use a well-placed lie to drive a wedge between Eve and her Creator. If you've ever been the victim of such a lie, you know how devastating it can be.

"Sara doesn't care about this fellowship anymore." In an attempt to discredit me the words were spoken about my wife by one the leaders in the church I was pastoring. They were far from the truth, for we had helped to plant the fellowship some 15 years earlier and loved the people as dear friends.

What made them sound believable was the truth in which the lie was embedded. "Wayne's been out of town for two Sundays and his wife didn't come to either Sunday morning service." While it was true that she had not been there, it was because she had been out of town helping my mother deal with an unexpected death in the family. She had cleaned house, helped with the funeral and lent her emotional support in my absence.

Nothing is more dangerous than taking that which is clearly true to prove a point that is not. Mixing a little lie with a lot of truth is like hiding cyanide in Kool Aid. You cannot tell it's there, until you drink it, but by then it is too late.

That's all the serpent needed to lull Adam and Eve into their nightmare. "You surely shall not die," was lie enough to deflect Eve's thinking. "We won't die?" she must have thought. "Then why would he tell us we would?" The enemy had his answer ready. "For God knows that when you eat of it your eyes will be opened, and you will be like God, knowing good and evil."

That last sentence is true, every word of it. God did know they would become like him in knowing good and evil and said so later. But notice how sinister these words become in the context of a lie. If they weren't really going to be harmed by eating the fruit, God was only doing it because he didn't want them to become like him. In other words, he was holding out on them.

There's the wedge. The God who made them, couldn't be trusted. He was too insecure, too threatened to let anyone else be like him. No longer certain of God's motives toward them, Adam and Eve could not trust him. Their relationship with God was now suspect; not something they valued, but something to work around to get what they were afraid God might not want for them. In other words, they acted in opposition to him, instead of in cooperation with him.

Not knowing who to believe, they did what they thought best. Seeing how delicious the fruit looked and wanting to be wise, they ate. At the root of all sin stands the same excuse: "I know best. I can get what I want on my own and not get hurt. Who needs God after all?"

The enemy had won, at least temporarily. He had violated the purity of God's new creation and severed the relationship between God and the people he loved. The effects of which we still feel thousands of years later. But the last word would not be the serpent's.

SOMETHING GREATER THAN OBEDIENCE

Imagine if Eve had known God well enough to trust his love

for her. How would she have responded to the serpent's charges against God?

I can see her face twisted in wonderment as she tries to hold back her laughter. "Are you talking about our God? The one who walked with us in the garden last night and who loves us so much that he has given us everything for our good. You're saying he would lie to us, because he doesn't want us to be like him? Absolutely, totally impossible! Not him. We are his children, after all!" And she could have walked away without even a second-thought. That's the kind of trust God wants us all to know.

If obedience had been the only issue with God, don't you think he would have made the whole scenario far clearer. He told them not to eat it or they would die. He didn't describe that death in detail. He could have told them how it would destroy his creation by bringing sin, disease, and relational brokenness into his world. It would cause them incredible pain, and not just for them but for all their offspring for thousands of years to come. He could have told them that all they needed to do was eat first of the Tree of Life, so that they would be eternally innocent in his presence.

But he didn't tell them. If he had they might have been obedient, but not because they trusted him. The would have obeyed only because it served their self-interest. God would merely have become a tool for their own fulfillment. Self would have still been at the center of their choice, and self would prevent them from discovering the full vitality of life in him. No, God didn't do it because he wanted something far better.

Neither did he interrupt the serpent to set the truth firmly in mind again. After all, he was there, wasn't he? Or do you imagine him busy in heaven with his back turned at that critical moment? We know now what Adam and Eve could not know then. They only recognized him when he cloaked himself in some physical manifestation and walked the garden with them. They didn't know that this God was present everywhere in his creation.

So why didn't he intervene? Could it be the same reason Jesus didn't send Peter home instead of letting him follow along to Caiaphas' courtyard and the betrayal that would surely follow? God sees something redemptive even in letting us fail. He seems less concerned about our mistakes than how we respond to them. Do they lead us away from trusting in our own strength or wisdom, to seek what it means to put our trust in him?

If so, then he finds our failures worth the pain they cause.

THE FINAL WORD

I'm sure the father of the prodigal could sit on the porch after his boy had returned, thinking that the money squandered in sin was well spent if it brought his son to the end of himself and into the relationship the father had always wanted with him. As painful as it was to watch, it had been necessary for the son to know exactly what kind of Father he had.

God could have helped Adam and Eve to make the right decision, certainly. But he wanted something else far more—to awaken the trust that would allow them to participate in the divine community. What an incredible plan! God provided a choice for them that was so obviously in their self-interest, but framed it in a way that seeking their own desires would lead them to the wrong choice. Only by learning to trust him would they experience the deepest longing of their heart.

Eden was not the final test. In God's heart it was only the first of many lessons. The familiar proverb tells us that if you love something set it free. If it comes back to you, it's yours. If it doesn't, it never was. Only those who have loved something enough to let it go can even get a glimpse of what God accomplished in that Garden.

God loved us that much and though many in the course of history have not come back many others have. Somehow the pain of those who do not is swallowed up in the joy of those who do. Thus the tragedy in the Garden becomes a stepping stone to the greater good he desired. In the midst of sin and selfishness, he would use our own waywardness and its consequences as the incubator in which our trust in his love might yet emerge.

That day began a process that would culminate at another tree—this one a cross on the hill at Golgotha. Here mercy would triumph over sin; and the trust that had been so illusive in that Garden for Adam and Eve would become certain for those who belong to God.

> For if, by the trespass of the one man, death reigned through that one man, how much more will those who receive God's abundant provision of grace and of the gift of righteousness reign in life through the one man, Jesus Christ.
>
> —ROMANS 5:17

For your personal journey

Ask God to reveal to you where wedges of mistrust have been inserted between you and him. Where do you find yourself doubting his love for you or his intentions with you? Where has trusting in your own abilities and wisdom taken you further from him rather than closer to him? Ask God to show you how to embrace a relationship with him his way and not your own.

Who Needed the Sacrifice?

Church! Why would I ever go there? I was already feeling terrible about myself. They'd just make me feel worse!
**A PROSTITUTE FROM CHICAGO AS QUOTED BY
PHILIP YANCEY IN *WHAT'S SO AMAZING ABOUT GRACE?***

"For God so loved the world that he gave his one and only Son, that whoever believes in him shall not perish but have eternal life" (John 3:16).

Am I the only one who didn't think this Scripture was such great news the first time I heard it? Yes, I know it speaks of an incredible gift God gave so that we would not have to perish for our sins. For us, it is undoubtedly a great thing. But what does it say about God?

When I heard this in Sunday School as a child, my first response was, "If he loved us so much, why didn't he do it himself?" Admittedly I might have been influenced by the chores I had to do at home: For Dad so loved a well-kept yard that he sent me out to mow it. Dad so loved his vineyard, that he sent me to work in it. Dad so loved an ice-cold Pepsi, that he sent me to the refrigerator to get it for him.

So why didn't God himself appear in human flesh and submit himself to the most painful and humiliating death imaginable? No, he sent the Son instead; or so I used to think. And my confusion didn't end there. While I was grateful for the salvation he provided, I had some concerns about God because of the way he provided it.

What kind of Father satisfies his need for justice by the death of his own Son? Couldn't he have just forgiven us without taking it out on an innocent victim? If someone wrongs me and the only way I could satisfy my anger was to punish someone else as the means to forgive them, what does that say about me?

If the cross served God's need to be appeased by a human sacrifice, especially that of his own Son, we are left with a host of disturbing questions. Raise them with others, and most will escape answering them by claiming that God's demand for justice is beyond our comprehension. But I am convinced the dissonant perspectives about God that result from an appeasement based view of the cross, cause many to shy away from the intimate relationship he seeks with us.

Instead the unanswerable questions should invite us to reconsider our distorted view of the cross. Since Adam's fall we have come to picture God not as a loving Father inviting us to trust him, but an exacting sovereign who must be appeased. When we start from that vantage point we miss God's purpose on the cross. For his plan was not to satisfy some need in himself at his Son's expense; but rather to satisfy a need in us at his own expense.

THE COVER-UP

Living by appeasement is a frightful game, especially when you play it with the all-knowing, Almighty God. Though I don't believe for a moment that God plays it, many of us were taught that he does and, thus, we alternate between trying to do enough to please him or trying to hide from him when we realize we can't.

The moment Adam and Even ate the fruit, their eyes were opened to see good and evil. The first evil they saw was in themselves. Though they had been naked since they were created, now they were aware of their nakedness and sought a cover-up for their shame.

Evidently the first thing they saw big enough to cover them were fig leaves. They plucked a few, sewed them together and slipped them on. I cringe at the thought. I've been in fig orchards and know how prickly and itchy those leaves are. As material for underwear it was a poor choice indeed; as are most of the ways we try to cover for ourselves.

But the real price of their shame is seen a short while later as God revealed himself again in the Garden. Instead of feeling safe with him, they felt compelled to run and hide. Notice that God did not hide from them. Neither was he angry at their disobedience. Instead he just showed up to be with them. They were the ones cowering in shame hoping the bushes would cover what the fig leaves couldn't.

As God came closer they told him of their shame and their failure. In doing so, they still sought cover. Adam blamed Eve; "the woman... gave me some fruit from the tree, and I ate it." No wonder they felt unsafe in their nakedness. They were. He turned on her to justify himself, using blame for the same purpose he had used fig leaves.

Adam's blame doesn't stop at Eve. It is not just the woman who tripped him up, but "the woman you put here with me." Adam even tried to pass some of the responsibility onto God. When God turns his attention to Eve, she blames the serpent's deception.

The creation was stained, and God parceled out the consequences of that failure. Already spiritually dead in the relational brokenness that resulted, their future physical death would follow. God threw them out of his Garden, not wanting them to eat from the Tree of Life and live forever in that sinful condition. By preserving eternity in holiness, God prepared a safe haven for their eventual rescue. "The soul that sins shall die," is a proclamation of mercy, not anger. It means that sin must have an end; and we an opportunity to regain what we forfeited.

TERMS OF APPEASEMENT

Their failure had profound consequences in the creation and in their relationship to their Creator. He could no longer be the friend who walked with them in the Garden, because their own sense of shame would cause them to cower whenever he approached.

Knowing good and evil didn't provide the joy Adam and Eve thought it would. Because they came to know good and evil outside of their trust in God, they had no power to resist evil and choose the good. They, and all generations after them, have found themselves captive to evil passions, with its destructive consequences and overwhelming sense of shame.

When God did make himself known, even the most righteous people fell on their faces, overwhelmed by their own unworthiness. The friendship he desired with his creation was thwarted. Instead of seeking his friendship, people only thought to appease him—doing enough good to somehow stay in his favor. The Creator had become someone to avoid not to embrace.

This shame so permeates our nature that this appeasement-based approach even emerged in every false religion humanity devised. From the earliest tribal attempts to appease the "gods of the earth" or the "god of rain" to more sophisticated religious systems with idolatry and tradition, the objective was always the same. What can we do to appease the wrath of the gods and find their favor?

He loves me, He loves me not.

Good times led to complacency and bad times to even greater rituals of repentant prayers, sacrificial offerings and good deeds. Their offerings started with small gestures of fruits or grain, but increasingly difficult times demanded ever-greater gifts. Soon animals were sacrificed, and in many cultures throughout the world eventually human sacrifice became the ultimate expression of commitment to their conception of god.

But this is not how the true God wanted to be known.

I WILL PROVIDE MY OWN

If you go to Tel Meggido in Israel today you can stand on an overlook and view an altar used to sacrifice first-born male children to the gods of the Canaanites. Your guide would tell you that that very altar was in use when Abraham came unto the Promised Land. They thought they could appease their false gods with such sacrifices.

Thus it was not so incredible for Abraham when the God who had touched his life had asked him to sacrifice his only son. All the other gods in Canaan did it, why not his? But this God was not a false god like the others interested in human sacrifice. This was the true and living God. He was going to reveal himself to Abraham and wanted him to know this God had nothing in common with Molech, Baal, or Asherah.

At God's word, Abraham took his son—a treasure born in his old age—and set out for Mt. Moriah. As they got close to the mountain, Isaac noticed that they had no sacrifice. "The fire and wood are here, but where is the lamb for the burnt offering?"

It appears that Abraham's response was less a brilliant insight into God's nature than it was a deflection to stave off the curiosity of his son. He nonetheless spoke prophetically the lesson God wanted to show him. "God himself will provide the lamb for the burnt offering, my son."

Only later, after his son lay tied to the altar and Abraham lifted the knife to plunge it into his son, did he see just how prophetic his words were. "Abraham! Abraham! Do not lay a hand on the boy . . . Do not do anything to him. Now I know that you fear God, because you have not withheld from me your son, your only son" (Genesis 22:12).

Abraham had faced the ultimate test in trusting his God. He discovered that God never wanted his son as a sacrifice at all. After God pointed out to Abraham a ram nearby caught in the bushes, he offered it in Isaac's place. Abraham declared that place "The Lord Will Provide" (Jehovah-jireh), understanding that his earlier words had proved more true than he could have imagined.

God drew a line that separated him from all the false gods

men have ever created. The false gods demanded sacrifices for their own appeasement. This God would provide the sacrifice we needed that could finally cover our shame and allow us to know him as he really is.

At Mt. Moriah God foreshadowed to Abraham what he would literally accomplish some three thousand years later on another hill not far away called Golgotha. It would not be the appeasement of an angry God by any sacrifice we could give, but an act of a loving God to sacrifice himself for those who were held captive in sin.

Far from being a blood-thirsty Sovereign demanding sacrifice to satiate his need for vengeance, the Living God spends himself to bring back the banished son or daughter. He did not need a sacrifice to love us; for he already did.

We needed a sacrifice for our shame so that we would be free to love him again. At the cross, God provided the undeniable proof of just how much he loves us. For those who understand that, it opens the door for us to do what Adam and Eve could not do that fateful day in the Garden—entrust our lives totally to the Living God.

> *Therefore, there is now no condemnation for those who are in Christ Jesus, because through Christ Jesus the law of the Spirit of life set me free from the law of sin and death.*
> —ROMANS 8:1-2

℞   ℞   ℞

For your personal journey

Can you recognize the effects of shame in your own life? What effort will you expend to make yourself look better to others, to yourself, or even to God? In your relationship with God do you think more of what you have to do for him or what he has already done for you? Ask him to show you how appeasement thinking distorts your relationship with him and ask him to free you from it so that you can participate in what he wants to do in you.

The Hen and Her Chicks

I had totally misunderstood the Christian faith.
I came to see that it was in my brokenness,
in my powerlessness, in my weakness that Jesus
was made strong. It was in the acceptance of
my lack of faith that God could give me faith.
MIKE YACONELLI QUOTED IN *ABBA'S CHILD*

The forest fire had been brought under control, and the fire-fighters were making sure all the hot spots had been extinguished. As they marched across the blackened landscape between the wisps of smoke still rising from the smoldering remains, a large lump on the trail caught a firefighter's eye.

As he got closer he noticed it was the charred remains of a large bird. Since birds can so easily fly away from the approaching flames, the firefighter wondered what was wrong with this bird that it could not escape. Had it been sick or injured?

Arriving at the carcass, he decided to kick it off the trail with his boot. As he did, however, he was startled by a flurry of activity around his feet. Four little birds flailed in the dust and ash, then scurried down the hillside.

The bulk of the mother's body had covered them from the searing flames. Though the heat was enough to consume her, it allowed her babies to find safety underneath. In the face of the rising flames, she had stayed with her young. She was their only hope for safety, and willing to risk her own life she gathered them together and covered them with her own body. Even when the pain reached its most unbearable moment, when she could easily have flown away to start another family on another day, she made herself stay through the raging flames.

Her dead carcass and her fleeing chicks told the story well enough—she gave the ultimate sacrifice to save her young. It also illustrates an even greater story—this one almost incomprehensible. In this story it is the Creator of heaven and earth who does exactly the same thing to rescue his wayward children from their own destruction.

THE WORST CURSE

Jesus was surrounded by his most hostile audience. No one gave him more trouble than the elders and Pharisees in Jerusalem. Their only priority seemed to be protecting their position in society and trying to deal with this miracle-working teacher with a mix of disdain one moment and feigned support when they were afraid of the people. To say they were the most disingenuous people he dealt with would be an understatement. They were always covering up their real motives and actions to act out a holiness they did not know.

In his final words to the city of Jerusalem, only days before his death, he exposes them for what they really are—hypocrites who turned the work of the loving God into a religion they manipulated for their own gain and sense of self-importance. Eight times he pronounced a curse on them, "Woe to you scribes, Pharisees and hypocrites." Five more times he calls them blind guides, or blind Pharisees.

He exposed them for keeping people from the reality of the kingdom; for making converts they only lured into greater bondage; for skewed priorities; for pretending to be righteous on the outside when evil raged within; for glorifying the prophets of the past and rejecting the prophets of their day.

The last charge was serious indeed. "You brood of vipers," Jesus called them, "how do you think you will escape the sentence of hell?" In the days ahead God would send his messengers to them again, but they would torture and kill them. Jesus warned them that because of their deeds they would be held responsible for "the guilt of all the righteous blood that has been shed on earth."

What a curse! They would be held accountable for the blood of every righteous person since the day Cain slew his brother, Abel. He could already see the consequences bearing down on them like a firestorm of wrath, seeking to consume them in their sin.

Don't these words seem completely out of character for Jesus? His message of love and forgiveness had captivated the land, drawing to him some of the most sinful people of his day. Yet these religious leaders he condemned in the cruelest of terms. Had he utterly rejected them?

That's what it appears on the surface, but look closer. Rather than taking delight in their coming devastation, he offered to risk his life to take part in their rescue. In words both poetic and poignant he makes them an incredible offer.

UNDER HIS WINGS

"O Jerusalem, Jerusalem, you who kill the prophets and stone those sent to you, how often I have longed to gather your children together, as a hen gathers her chicks under her wings, but you were not willing."
—MATTHEW 23:37

They had rejected God and the messengers he had sent. They had earned the harshest of sentences for their actions and yet Jesus still wanted to draw them to himself and bear the destruction for them. Their city would be conquered and their children devastated by the consequences of living selfishly instead of trusting in the Living God.

Jesus invoked the same image the firefighter had seen in the woods. He presented himself as a hen trying to gather chicks to herself. That only happens when danger presses in upon them. A hen doesn't nurse her children or cuddle them to sleep. But when a predator comes near or the coop catches on fire she will try to gather them under her wings. Pulling them beneath her she will cover them with her body, risking her own life for their safety.

Jesus could see the firestorm their own sin had produced approaching Jerusalem. It would devour them utterly. Even though many in that crowd would cry for his crucifixion only a few days later, he still wanted them. Like the hen, he offered them a safe place under his wings, willing to endure the fire to the point of death to rescue whoever wanted to come.

When it would have been so easy for him to abandon them to the fate they deserved, he was going to stay and meet the approaching fire in its full fury. What must it take for a bird to stay over her babies as the fire draws ever-closer, then begins to sear her neck and back? What must it have taken for God himself to endure the fury of the wrath our sins deserved and stay through it to the end so that those under his wings might be saved?

"But you were not willing." The story's end was tragic for those who stood around Jesus that day. Unwilling to come to him they would have to endure the fire themselves to its tragic end. I doubt there are words that break Father's heart more than these. After all he had done to deliver them from the ravages of sin, they were unwilling.

Not all chicks run to their mothers in time of danger. Some, either paralyzed in panic or trying to find a way to save themselves, are devoured. She cannot run around gathering them individually. They have to come to her. That's all the young chicks in the forest fire had done to be safe. They didn't have to earn it; all they had to do was run under the mother's wing and let her cover them.

Those who did were rescued; those who didn't were devoured. It didn't matter if they thought they had a better idea.

It didn't matter if they thought they could outrun it. All that mattered was their willingness to trust the call of their mother.

Most of Jerusalem on that day would not accept Jesus' call and would face the terrible judgment ahead on their own terms. But the story doesn't have to end that way for you. If you want, you can give up all the ways you try to save yourself and come running to him. He will pull you up close, under his wing and take for you what you could never endure.

UNLIMITED PATIENCE

Look how closely our choice in Christ parallels Adam and Eve's choice in the Garden. If they had trusted their Creator's love for them, they would not have had to resort to their own means to become like God. Once they doubted his love for them, they could only fall back on their best wisdom, which proved woefully inadequate.

The elders in Jerusalem faced a similar choice. Would they trust their own religious ways to save themselves, or would they trust God's work in Jesus? Remember these were not self-indulgent men fulfilling their passions by outwardly sinful acts. No, the deception for them was much like it was for Adam and Eve. These were men trying to be godly, or so they thought. They observed cumbersome rituals and traditions thinking that would make them like God. They spurned the pleasures of the world in an effort to earn his approval. But being good wasn't good enough.

They were still engaged in an attempt to save themselves, and they would end up in the same mess as Adam and Eve. No matter how righteous they could be on the outside, it would bring them no closer to God. They were still trusting themselves, instead of him.

Jesus unmasked that most clearly when he called one of their own to himself. Paul, formerly called Saul, had grown up training to be a Pharisee. Everything about his life conformed to their code, such that Paul could later say that no one was his equal in zeal for God and as to legalistic righteousness, he was faultless. With such impressive credentials, you would think him well-placed for God's work.

Rubbish! That's what Paul called that way of thinking. It was boasting in the flesh, he said, and that flesh had not saved him. It had only driven his sin ever deeper underground. Though he appeared to be one of the most righteous men in his day, in reality he was full of sin. He called himself the worst of sinners, because his religious exterior had only been a cover-up for the sin that destroyed him from within. He calls himself a "blasphemer and a persecutor and a violent man."

Don't mistake his assessment here as the mere humility of a gracious man. Paul is trying to convince all who would listen that self-righteousness is no righteousness at all. Driven by his desire to be one of the spiritual elite of his day, he had only found himself in greater sin. When Jesus found him, he was in fact killing God's people thinking he was doing God's work.

Why did Jesus save Paul? In Paul's words, "I was shown mercy so that in me, the worst of sinners, Christ Jesus might display his unlimited patience as an example for those who would believe on him and receive eternal life" (1 Tim. 1:16).

I've sat with people convinced they were far too evil for God to want them. I've often referred to this passage, asking them if they had done worse than Paul had done and haven't ever had someone tell me they had. God saved Paul, so the most broken, devastated and sinful person would feel free to come running under his wing. All they have to do is come.

A REAL COVERING

When God put Adam and Eve out of the Garden, he even looked in mercy at their cover-up. Taking the undergarments they had fashioned from the fig leaf collection, he made them clothing of animal skins. It was not only an act of mercy, but also prophetic demonstration. The blood shed to cover them that day, testified to a future day when Jesus' death would provide the covering we really need.

Shame craves for a covering. We've already seen how it can reveal itself in blaming others, even God, for our own choices and weaknesses. Now we see how shame can use religion to the same end. We live in a world where everybody covers up to protect themselves. That's why relationships in religious environments can turn so painful when people have to tear others down to make themselves look better.

We push to achieve beyond our peers so we can feel superior to them. We blame others so we don't have to face our own weaknesses. We gossip about the failures of others so we can feel better about ourselves. We even look for religious institutions to affirm us so that we can ignore the doubts that assail us.

It seems we are all on the relentless pursuit to hide our own inadequacies and seek our own security. In doing so, we are like little chickens running around the burning coop throwing leaves over our heads hoping they will be enough.

But they won't be. There is only one covering that will save us from ourselves; and it is Jesus himself. He endured the firestorm for us so that those who crawl under his wings can dwell in safety. He is the only covering that at once delivers us from our shame and frees us from the bondage of sin.

Cover yourself in him. Learn to live under his wings today and every day for the rest of your life. How do you do that? By learning to trust him completely in every situation you face.

Of course that is far easier said than done. When difficulties press in around us, we are most likely to doubt God's motives towards us. Could that be the voice of the serpent still whispering in our ears? "If God's not going to give you what you think you need, maybe you should go get it yourself."

Trusting our own wisdom is so easy we find ourselves doing it before we ever realize it. There is only one place where we can learn the trust in God that was shattered in Eden—at the cross of Jesus Christ. His willingness to trade his life for stands as unmistakable evidence of his love for you.

When you understand what really happened there, then you will know how much you are loved. When you know how much you're loved you'll find trusting him to be as easy as breathing.

> *May I never boast except in the cross of our Lord Jesus Christ, through which the world has been crucified to me, and I to the world.*
> —GALATIANS 6:14

❦   ❦   ❦

For your personal journey

Where do you try to save yourself using your own ingenuity to survive, rather than trusting Jesus to lead you as he desires? Isn't his unlimited patience amazing and that even after our worst deeds, he stands ready to cover us with his wings and let us abide safely in him. Ask him to show you what that specifically means for you and to teach you how to live every day and through every circumstance trusting that he loves you.

14

What Really Happened on the Cross

"What changed these very ordinary men (who were such cowards that they did not dare stand too near the cross in case they got involved) into heroes who would stop at nothing? A swindle? Hallucination? Spooky nonsense in a darkened room? Or Somebody quietly doing what he said he'd do—walk right through death?"
J. B. PHILLIPS, *IS GOD AT HOME?*

The events on earth have been well-documented. All of the writers of the gospels tell of his inquisition before the religious leaders of Jerusalem, his trial before Pilate, his scourging by Roman soldiers, and his crucifixion on a cross. The humiliation and physical torture of death by crucifixion has been the subject of many sermons and books. We know well the agony he endured by being nailed to a cross with a crown of thorns pressed into his scalp and we also know how his agony intensified over the three hours he hung exposed in public view, mocked by his detractors.

The significance of that moment, however, is not so easy to understand. The appeasement-based view of the cross that most of us have understood goes something like this: Because Jesus lived a sinless life he did not deserve to die. However, he submitted himself to his Father's desire and as a sacrifice the guilt of our sins was laid upon him. Therefore God gave him the punishment our sins deserved. Our sentence has been satisfied with God so that we are now absolved for our sins and can stand justified before Almighty God.

Though this scenario may satisfy our inherent sense of shame for our own sins and failures, it only tells part of the story. If we go no further, this appeasement-based view of the cross describes Father and Son playing a divine version of good cop/bad cop. To keep the demanding judge of the universe from executing the full weight of his wrath on us, Jesus rushed onto the scene and threw himself in the way. God's wrath destroyed him and thus mollified his anger.

But that is only an earthly view of that incredible event. Scripture is laced with glimpses at a far fuller perspective. Here we see what happened *in God*—the work a Father and Son accomplished together, not to appease God's anger, but to cleanse us of sin. Their plan was not to punish sin, but destroy its power and offer a way for humanity to be rescued from the dregs of sin and recapture the relationship God had always wanted with his people.

What we see from his vantage point is not the story of a punished victim, but something far more magnificent.

NOT JUST A VICTIM

Yes, Jesus was brutally tortured and it was certainly the intent of the Roman guard that the extreme tortures used against him would end his life. That, however, is not the whole story. Nothing they could do would have been sufficient to kill the Son of God.

Jesus was neither a victim of the lies of the religious rulers nor of Rome's corrupt political posturing. No amount of torture would have been sufficient to kill him. Death would only come when he surrendered to it. "The reason my Father loves me is that I lay down my life... No one takes it from me, but I lay it down of my own accord" (John 10:17-18).

Only the soul that sins, dies. Since Jesus knew no sin, death could not overpower him. Instead he submitted to it for a greater good. He didn't just submit to the events of the cross, but even at its end he yielded his spirit into God's hands and gave himself over to death.

Neither Adam and Eve in the Garden, nor Christ on the cross were victims of other people's choices. In the pristine beauty of the undefiled Creation, Adam and Eve couldn't find it in their hearts to trust God and walk away from their own desires. But in the agonizing atrocity of the cross and the utter darkness that overwhelmed him there, Jesus consciously and continuously yielded to his Father's desire.

At any point in the process he could have stopped the torture, called for a legion of angels and wiped out those who were killing him. What an amazing act! I don't know that I have ever willingly submitted to the darkest tragedies of my life. I rarely feel in control when circumstances turn desperate or when people with evil motives take advantage of me. If I could have called a legion of angels to fix any of my painful circumstances, I would have. I have endured the painful seasons of my life, not because I chose to, but because I couldn't do otherwise. The only choice I had was whether to respond to them in a Godly way or a selfish way.

That he would endure such hostility against himself with the full freedom to end it at any weak moment, makes me appreciate the cross that much more. As free choice got us into this bondage of sin, so Jesus' free choice would walk us out of it. His example also reminds us that we are not victims either. Even though disgusting things might be done to us by others, we still have the freedom to overcome evil by putting our trust in him. He still redeems the darkest moments of life with the wonder of his grace.

NOT JUST JESUS...

I'll be the first to admit that the relationship between Father, Son and Spirit is a mystery beyond our ability to define with absolute certainty. But I am deeply bothered by the thought that in some way God was able to separate himself at the cross. The popular understanding of the cross seems to be that God the Father executed wrath on God the Son while standing at some discrete distance.

Such thinking not only denies the essence of God's nature but then distorts what happened at the cross. Paul wrote that "God was reconciling the world to himself in Christ..." God was no distant observer, but a participant. He didn't send Jesus to do what he would not do; but God himself acted through Jesus to bring about our redemption.

Some have taken Jesus' cry that his Father had forsaken him to mean that at the darkest moment, the Father had to turn his back on the Son. God cannot bear to look on sin, they argue, so that when our sins were laid on him, God had to turn his face away from his Son.

Never mind that God has never run from sinful humanity. He didn't hide from Adam and Even in the Garden. *They* hid from him as *he* sought them out. It is not God who cannot bear to look on sin, but that we in our sin can't bear to look on God. He's not the one who hides, we are. God is powerful enough to look on sin and be untainted by it. He has always done so. He did so at the cross.

In Chapter 16 we'll take a closer look at why Jesus cried out, "My God, my God, why have you forsaken me!" The point here is that all of God was fully involved in all aspects of this incredible plan. The anguish that ripped through the Godhead that day cannot even be fathomed by our limited perspective.

But it is important that we see them working together, enduring the process necessary to destroy sin and liberate those they loved. Jesus was not the victim and his Father the victimizer. They were executing a plan they—the Father, Son and Spirit—had devised on the day they first decided to create a man and a woman. They would pay the price together for the relationship they so deeply desired to share.

NOT JUST GUILTY OF SIN

*"God made him who had no sin to be sin for us, so
that in him we might become the righteousness of God."*
—2 CORINTHIANS 5:21

To say that God laid the guilt of our sins on Jesus so that he could punish him misses the larger point. Jesus wasn't just guilty of our sins; he *became* sin itself. Notice the word is in the singular, not talking about the *acts* of sin, but the very root of it—that self-preferring, self-trusting nature that puts itself above God.

Paul wrote that in a moment in time God made Jesus the personification of sin. While that may appear only as a minor subpoint at first glance, it is critical if we are going to understand what really happened on that cross. He didn't just deal with our sins, but with the very nature of sin itself.

By allowing sin to touch his person through the Son, he would be able to prevail in himself over that which we were powerless to fight. Through the physical body of Jesus, sin came face to face with the power of God, and as we shall see, God prevailed over sin completely.

This underscores the fallacy of any law-based or performance-based approach to God. Jesus became sin for us precisely because we were powerless to deal with it ourselves. Scripture is clear here. If any of us could have been righteous on our own, then there would have been no need for Jesus to die. When we fell into sin in a state of unbelief in who God was, sin became an inescapable trap. We couldn't win over it without trust, and we couldn't trust while blinded by sin.

Thus God takes sin into himself through the physical body of Jesus and accomplishes what the law never could—"he condemned sin in sinful man" (Rom. 8:3). Notice it's not sinful people here who are condemned, but the sin within them. The reason we are free from condemnation in Jesus, is because he condemned sin in himself. It could not prevail over God's power, and by breaking its power, he opened the door for all who want to be set free of it and live in the life of the Father.

NOT JUST PUNISHMENT

Notice how God's perspective doesn't focus on our sins as much as it does the power of sin itself. This is critical. For the cross was not just an act of punishment for sin. It wasn't just Jesus stepping forward as an innocent victim to take our place on the gallows. Certainly that image does express some of what happened, but punishment alone doesn't break the power of sin.

We see that in our own society. Children punished for wrong doing, often only find a better way to hide it next time or, despite their best efforts, fall victim to it again. So many people who serve jail time for an offense, find themselves back again within a short time of being freed. Don't we all know that the desires of our flesh are often stronger than threat of punishment or negative consequence?

No, the cross was not primarily about exacting punishment; it was about prevailing over sin's power. In the Son God didn't just punish sin, but he served up the antidote that Christ was able to endure until sin itself was destroyed.

Now, all who embrace him can live in the effects of that antidote, prevailing over sin through a growing relationship to the Creator of all.

God made him who had no sin to be sin for us, so that in him we might become the righteousness of God.
—2 CORINTHIANS 5:21

For your personal journey

What comes first to your mind as you contemplate the death of Jesus? Think beyond the physical realities and see what transpired between Father and Son, as they provided a safe place for you from the destruction of sin itself. There is nothing more to do here than to simply express to God our gratefulness for providing such an incredible gift.

The Antidote for Sin

If you love deeply, you're going to get hurt badly.
But it's still worth it.
C.S. Lewis in *Shadowlands*

It was the most poignant picture of wrath I've witnessed. I had taken my family camping in the Sierra Nevada mountains to escape the heat of our home on the valley floor and to soak in some rest and relaxation. I was hunkered down in a lounge chair deeply engrossed in a novel. My wife, Sara, was coming to join me when suddenly we heard screams of pain from our two-year-old son, Andy.

He'd been playing in the dirt not far from our campsite. As I looked up he was stomping his feet and waving his hands wildly. Swirling around him were flying insects, backlit by the sun, Sara immediately recognized as bees. Somehow he had stumbled into their nest in the ground and they were attacking him relentlessly.

Before I could extricate myself from the reclining chair, Sara had already rushed to the sounds of his screams. Even though she is allergic to bee stings and got stung for her efforts, she angrily swatted at the bees as she scooped up her son to run with him to safety. When I got to them she was stroking his head with comfort while still panting from the overload of adrenaline still coursing through her veins. Soon she reacted to the venom and we took her to the hospital for treatment.

If you want a picture of God's wrath, I can think of none better. She was as angry as I've ever seen her, but the anger wasn't directed at Andy nor did it seek retribution. She simply risked herself to rescue someone she loved so deeply.

THE WRATH OF GOD

That's what God's wrath is like. He sees the evil that mars his creation and destroys people he loves and he must be rid of it. His wrath consumes evil and wickedness and as such does not exist as the opposite of his love, but as an expression of that love. It must protect and set free the object of his affection.

I'm sure when my son first saw mom running at him eyes blazing with anger, he thought he was in trouble. Even though he didn't know what he'd done wrong, he was already recoiling from her as she approached. Only after she had swept him to safety did he realize he was not in trouble.

I think our shame-consciousness toward God does the same thing. Whenever we see God acting to consume sin, we internalize the anger against ourselves. But that isn't where the wrath is primarily directed. "The wrath of God is being revealed from heaven against all the godlessness and wickedness of men…" (Rom. 1:18).

It's not people that God seeks to destroy but the sin that destroys his people. In that sense God's wrath is far more curative than it is punitive. It's primary purpose is not to hurt us, but heal and redeem us.

That's not to say that God's wrath doesn't ultimately devour people as well. Often in the scriptures, God's consuming presence spelled the end of people's lives who were so given over to evil and wickedness that the two could no longer be separated. Wrath, therefore, as it consumed sin also consumed the people who had become so ensnared by it that were no longer interested in reaching out to God's mercy.

Israel only occupied the Promised Land because the nations before them had been so given over to evil that they were unredeemable. That's why God didn't give the land to Abraham, but waited until the full measure of their sin had been realized. Then he gave it to the children of Israel.

Isn't it interesting that at the end of Revelation, even those who know they have dishonored the living God, curse him instead of repenting? It seems God will use the catastrophic events of the last days to so polarize society, that all those who would come to him would have full opportunity to do so. And those that don't, will not be able to claim later that they had no idea who he was.

Notice that the purpose of this wrath is to consume sin and cleanse the universe. That's what it does; first inside of us if we'll let it but if not, it will do away with us. For sin must be consumed by wrath.

THE CUP JESUS DID NOT WANT

"My Father, if it is possible, may this cup be taken from me." This is the substance of Jesus' agonizing prayer prayed over and over again in his own Garden on the eve of his crucifixion. The words are interesting. What cup is he talking about?

Certainly he could simply be using cup as a metaphor for the difficult circumstances that lay ahead of him. But Scripture also speaks about God's wrath being in a cup that is consumed by those who have been devoured by sin. Perhaps a verse from Revelation expresses it best. Those who worship the beast will "drink of the wine of God's fury, which has been poured full strength into the cup of his wrath" (Rev. 14:10).

Could this be the cup that Jesus resisted that evening? Could the thought of being the object of his own Father's wrath be so unbearable to contemplate that he sought another means to effect salvation? I don't know that it is so, for Scripture does not say it in so many words; but I think it is likely.

If it is God's wrath that consumes sin, and if the redemptive plan was to consume sin in sinful flesh, then it could be that Jesus drank from that same cup. This would have made the physical tortures of the cross pale in comparison. In those hours he hung on the cross, he drank from God's cup so that the wrath of God might consume sin in the Son.

Thus God's wrath is not just punishment for sin, it is also antidote to it. By destroying sin it opened the door to a future world without it. As God's wrath will eventually purge the world of sin, so it could also purge the sin in us. The only problem is that in our fallen state, God's wrath would consume us before it would consume our sin. For us it's a case of the cure being worse than the disease. Whenever God's wrath broke out in the Old Testament to consume sin, people died! The flesh was too weak to withstand the cleansing.

But before the beginning of the world, Father and Son had devised a plan together that could redeem the object of their affection.

DRINKING THE CUP

What if you had a young child who was diagnosed with a rare blood disease. As the doctors tell you about it, they tell you that the disease is almost unheard of in children. Though they have a form of chemotherapy that could cleanse your child's blood and restore him to health, the drug is too strong for the child's undeveloped body to withstand the dose necessary to cure him. In other words, the cure would kill him before it healed him.

But there is a way around that, they say. They could administer the chemotherapy into your blood. Though it would make you deathly ill and possibly even kill you, the therapy could produce antigens in your blood that could then be transplanted to your child's body and cleanse him of the disease as well. Would you do it? Most parents wouldn't hesitate for a second.

Neither did God. This was his opportunity to destroy the power of sin and liberate those who had been captives to it all their lives. The onlookers at Golgotha that day only saw a man experiencing the agonizing death of crucifixion. They did not know that the sinless one had been made sin for them and that the physical pains of the cross only reflected in human terms what transpired in God's eternity.

It seems that the cup of wrath was lifted to his lips and Jesus drank of it fully, letting it eat away at sin itself. He drank it to the end letting wrath war against sin until sin succumbed to the power of God and was consumed in him.

How can we even imagine the battle that ravaged his soul during those hours? We have glimpses of it certainly, but only that. Jesus not only entered the utter depths of the pain, darkness, shame, and anguish to which sin can drive humanity, but he also endured the full weight of God's being warring against that sin to its utter destruction.

The first we can relate to in part because we have all tasted of sin and its painful and destructive consequences. The latter we will never have to know if we will let his death be our own. For he has already borne in himself what we could never have borne and survived. He endured such hostility against himself because he was committed to our freedom from the power of sin.

When I consider just how unfair it might have been for God to have created that tree in Eden that caused so much grief and pain, I only have to look at the cross. Why could he put that tree there? Because he had already determined that he would pay the greatest price for the stumbling block it would be for Adam and Eve. Even in giving us the freedom to trust him or trust ourselves, God already knew that he would suffer the most for that choice. Somehow to him, the glory of fellowship with his created ones outweighs any price he had to pay to experience it.

By enduring to the end, sin was fully conquered in him. Its spell over humanity was broken and no longer does anyone have to be consumed by sin itself, nor God's wrath against it. The antidote had not only worked in him, by doing so it had produced in his blood a fountain of life as well. Transfused into any person who desires it, his blood can cleanse us of sin and reunite us with God himself—fulfilling the dream that he had when he first decided to create man and woman and place them in the center of his creation.

He Loves Me!

THIS CUP'S FOR YOU

"This cup is the new covenant in my blood, which is poured out for you" (Luke 22:20).

Only a few hours before as he shared a final meal with his disciples, Jesus spoke of the cup he would provide for us. Having drunk of the cup of wrath our sins deserved and having used that to condemn sin in sinful flesh, now he offers us a different cup. This cup is filled with his blood that has been purified and teems with life and grace.

Now he invites you to come and drink of his cup as the antidote that can cleanse not only the sins of your past, but sin itself that wars in your heart and holds you captive to its desires. He has broken the bondage if you will come and drink of him.

Unlike the fall in Eden that subjected every one of us and the earth itself to the captivity of sin; this gift freely given, must be freely received. God's desire for us to enter into relationship with him is still based on our choice.

Though he pursues us with an undying love and offers us to drink of the fountain of life, he will not make any of us come.

This is your choice pure and simple.

The door is open; all we have to do is trust him enough to walk through it. There's that word again—trust! What Adam and Eve did not do in the Garden, we can now do through the work of the cross.

Enduring the antidote for sin was only part of it.

Something else happened on that cross that was meant to change our lives forever.

> *In him we have redemption through his blood, the forgiveness of sins, in accordance with the riches of God's grace that he lavished on us with all wisdom and understanding.*
>
> —EPHESIANS 1:7-8

For your personal journey

Do you see God's wrath directed at sin, or directed at you? It is one thing to say God loves the sinner and hates the sin, but sometimes we feel that God is out to get us as well. Wherever you see that in your thinking, ask God to help you change your mind and see things the way he does. He wants you to know that everything he has done in your life is to bring you into the fullness of his love. Where you don't understand that, ask him to show you.

In the Darkest Moment...Trust

You will trust God only as much as you love him. And you will love him not because you have studied him; you will love him because you have touched him—in response to his touch...Only if you love will you make that final leap into darkness. "Father, into your hands I commend my spirit."

BRENNAN MANNING IN *LION AND LAMB*

When the enemy drove a wedge between Eve and her Creator, he had won the moment. Everything we do as a result of not trusting God and his intentions toward us result in everdeepening bondage to sin. That's as true of indulging our selfish desires as it is trying to appease him.

This is where an appeasement view of the cross serves us so poorly. By viewing the cross as the offer of a "Get-Out-Of-Hell-Free Card" rather than an invitation of friendship with a gracious Father, we empty it of its power. By preying on people's uncertainty about the afterlife we can get them to go forward, pray a sinner's prayer or whatever else we ask them to do to ensure they go to heaven.

But then our problem only begins. Most go right back to living the way they had before, hopeful that they did enough not to worry about hell any longer. Some will get involved in a religious group or activity as an expression of their sincerity to God, but they will all soon discover that the reality of Christianity doesn't live up to its promise. They'll still find themselves overwhelmed by sin too great to conquer because they have not let him deal with the root of it.

For the power of the cross to significantly change our lives it would have to restore the trust that was shattered in Eden.

And that it does in spectacular fashion.

FORSAKEN SON?

Perhaps Jesus' most puzzling words from the cross was his cry of utter loneliness and despair, "My God, my God, why have you forsaken me?" Theologians have grappled with those words for centuries trying to sort out what was happening between Father and Son at that moment.

Could the Faithful One be unfaithful to his Son? Of course not. Even when Jesus told his disciples that they would all leave him alone, he said he would not be alone for the Father was with him. I don't believe for a minute that the Father forsook the Son. But there could be a vast difference here between what God *did* and what Jesus *perceived*. Jesus undoubtedly felt forsaken but that doesn't mean that he was.

Perhaps Psalm 22 holds a clue here since Jesus used the exact same words that David penned there. Read these excerpts from that Psalm as David vacillates between his security in God's love and his fear that he had lost it:

- "My God, my God, why have you forsaken me? ...Yet you are enthroned as the Holy One."

- "I cry out by day, but you do not answer... Yet, our fathers...trusted and you delivered them."

- "But I am a worm and not a man, scorned by men and despised by the people...Yet you brought me out of the womb; you made me trust in you..."

- "I am poured out like water, and all my bones are out of joint... (Yet) he has not hidden his face from him but has listened to his cry for help."

David eloquently described the torrent of emotions that sin produces in us, overwhelming us with emptiness and making us feel abandoned. But he also affirms that God is there nonetheless and in the end will have his way even through our agony.

When Jesus became sin for us he entered into the full shame, darkness and bondage of that sin. It is likely at the moment on the cross when God's wrath was consuming the sin he had become, that he couldn't even see the Father with whom he had shared fellowship through all eternity. Sin blinded him and he felt as if God had forsaken him. But that is the difference between the perception of sin and the reality of God.

We too feel abandoned by God at some of our darkest moments. It doesn't mean he's left us, only that we can't see him through the darkness. The resounding truth, however, is that God is always there, never turning his face against those who are his. To believe he did so with Christ is unthinkable.

That Jesus felt abandoned only shows the depth to which he experienced our sin. He entered into it fully and for a moment in eternity the Son knew what it was like to experience Fatherlessness. How painful that must have been since he had lived every moment with his eye on his Father. He might even have lost sight of the purpose of the cross itself, so utterly dark is the depth of sin.

Unseen though he was, the Father was still there in the same measure that he had always been. But having become sin itself; he could no longer sense his Father's presence. Perception would become its own reality as Jesus shared in the emptiness and loneliness that perhaps defines hell itself. There is a mystery here far deeper than Scripture clarifies and we must take care not to make too much of it. But it seems that in allowing sin to touch the Godhead, it caused a rift in the divine community. The price of our sin was borne in their wounding. How his cry must have ripped at his Father's heart, thinking him the object of separation rather than love.

But the story didn't end there.

OUT OF THE DEPTHS

It is not long after his cry of abandonment comes the greatest demonstration of trust in the history of the world.

"Father into your hands I commit my spirit."

To the Father he could not see.

To fulfill a plan that had long since faded from view.

In utter despair and loneliness, Jesus did what Adam and Eve could not do living in the most pristine and beautiful of gardens.

He trusted his Father.

He committed his entire being into his Father's hands and in doing so breathed his last. The horror of the cross had reached its end. Sin had been consumed and his body spent. But his dying breath affirmed a heart of trust beyond comprehension. Now death's barrier had been crossed in a state of absolute trust and surrender. The power of death would be conquered, too.

Paul affirms repeatedly that God's work at the cross stands as the undeniable proof that we are loved. That God would go to such lengths to rescue us from our own waywardness so that we might be his friend forever secures God's motive concerning each of us. "Very rarely will anyone die for a righteous man... but God demonstrates his own love for us in this: While we were still sinners, Christ died for us" (Rom. 5:7-8).

Whether it's the hen covering the chicks against the encroaching flames or the mother rushing into a bee swarm to scoop up her child, once love is demonstrated to that degree how can it be doubted any longer? By inserting himself between us and our destruction God wanted us to know that we could trust him about anything. When the reality of the cross sinks home, the enemy's wedge is dislodged.

No longer do we need to hesitate to trust this incredible

Father and his intentions toward us, especially when we lose sight of what God is doing in our lives, or question his seeming inactivity. Instead of doubting him, we can assume he's doing something greater than our expectations might allow for and continue to walk with him instead of separating our self from him.

Not only does the cross demonstrate God's willingness to love us at the ultimate personal cost, but Jesus also modeled for us how we can live in that trust—"...into your hands I commit my spirit." When I can't figure out what God is doing; when I've just messed up to the greatest degree; when I'm lonely and empty, the answer is still the same, "...into your hands I commit my spirit."

THE FAITH OF JESUS

The heritage of the cross is a life lived in trust. It takes us from the bondage of sin that feels less loved and is always compensating for it to knowing that we are loved by the God of the universe. This is the faith we are called to live by and it is not even our own.

Few versions of the Bible translate Galatians 2:20 exactly as it appears in the original Greek. Paul wrote: "I have been crucified with Christ and I no longer live, but Christ lives in me. The life I live in the body, I live by *the* faith *of* the Son of God, who loved me and gave himself for me."

The vast majority translate it, "...the life I live in the body, I live by faith *in* the Son of God." They cannot conceive of what Paul might have meant by living by the faith of Jesus. So they translate it as "faith in the Son of God" since a number of other scriptures talk about the importance of putting our faith in him. But Paul is talking about something different here. There is no ambiguity in the original language about the distinction between where our faith might be directed and to whom it belongs. It is clearly the latter. In other words, Paul is saying he lives off of Jesus' faith, not by mustering up enough of his own.

What great encouragement that provides! How often do you feel weak in faith? Try as hard as you might to believe, belief still escapes you. How do you muster up what you already lack? While they may be right, it is rarely helpful when people tell us we just need to trust Jesus more. Of course that's true, but how do I trust him more than I already do?

The answer lies here. Paul saw his life ending when Christ's ended at the cross. He didn't even live by his own human faith after that. He let Jesus live in him. He let Jesus' trust in the Father stand for his.

My wife and I have done that as well. In the most severe trials of our journey, we have held each other in the storm; at times paralyzed by circumstances beyond our ability to endure. Sometimes with tear-stained faces we have simply prayed, "Jesus we choose to believe in the Father's love for us because you did. Give us your faith to stand right here and trust you."

It's amazing how that simple act works in us. It releases a power beyond our own abilities or intellect. Our eyes see a bit more clearly; our heart finds greater endurance. Answers we thought we needed no longer seem important. His presence and purpose alone prove sufficient in the storm. Eventually we come to recognize his hand doing something greater in our lives than we had hoped for at the time.

A LIFE LIVED IN TRUST

The apostle John told us that that was the secret to living in this kingdom. He said he wrote his gospel so that those who read it would "believe that Jesus is the Christ, the Son of God, and that by believing you may have life in his name" (John 20:30-31).

We have cheapened this verse with the popular notion that believing Jesus is the Christ is an affirmation of correct doctrine. If one gives mental assent to the fact that Jesus is the Christ then one has his life. That's not what John was talking about. The word we translate *believe* is simply the verb form of faith. Perhaps the word *trust* would bring out his fuller meaning.

John was not encouraging people to confess the right creed, but inviting them to learn what God started to teach us in the Garden—how to trust him completely. John chose the events he did from Jesus' life so that we might be stirred to trust who he is and by living in that trust every day, to experience the life of God. We don't enter into this kingdom by a sinner's prayer, going forward at a religious gathering or reciting an orthodox creed but by learning to trust who he is and by living in that trust every day.

Those who do, discover God's life, even here in a broken and fallen world. What God accomplished in Christ on the cross not only defeated our sin but allows us to build a life of trust. He loves you absolutely and completely and will every day of your life on this planet and into the age to come.

The moment Jesus yielded to death on the cross God's victory over sin and death was assured. What happened three days later only ratified the work he'd already finished. God raised him from the dead because he had already conquered it in his wholehearted trust in his Father and as the firstborn of a whole new race of men and women.

Now we can live as loved people. No longer oppressed by the need to appease God we are free to live in his love and as we'll see, that can completely transform everything about the way we think and live.

> *I have been crucified with Christ and I no longer live, but Christ lives in me. The life I live in the body, I live by faith in the Son of God, who loved me and gave himself for me.*
>
> —GALATIANS 2:20

For your personal journey

Where is it easy for you to trust God, and where is it difficult? How can Jesus' example encourage you to trust God when he seems the most distant from you? Since it is his faith we want to live by, ask Jesus to teach you how to grow in trust and how to fix your hope on him in a way that runs deeper than your circumstances or feelings.

A Life Lived in Love

For Christ's love compels us, because we are

convinced that one died for all, and therefore all died.

And he died for all, that those who live should no

longer live for themselves but for him who died

for them and was raised again.

—2 Corinthians 5:14-15

Trying to Earn Points With Someone Who Is No Longer Keeping Score

God is not disillusioned with you, because he had no illusions about you in the first place.
GERALD COATES IN UNPUBLISHED COMMENTS

For my dear friend, the words came with great pain. For me, they signaled an incredible breakthrough in my own relationship with God. The juxtaposition couldn't have been stranger.

In the last few months he had watched his wife grow more distant and threaten to leave him. He had done everything he could to prove his love to her and to let her know that he would be willing to change anything to save their relationship.

But none of it had worked—not the new car he bought her, not the change in jobs she'd requested, not even his persistent words of entreaty. That morning she had left. He looked at me through teary eyes, "Wayne, I have come to realize that I have been trying to earn points with someone who was no longer keeping score."

In his situation I cannot imagine more painful words. My heart broke for him, and we spent the rest of our lunch together sorting out his options and finding out how I could support him in the difficult days ahead.

His words, however, had touched something far deeper and had coalesced in a simple phrase what the Father had been working into my life over the previous months. What had borne tragic news to him had signaled new-found freedom for me. I had spent all of my life in the faith doing with God what he had done with his wife. I, too, had been trying to earn points with someone who was no longer keeping score, though for far different reasons.

My friend's wife had stopped keeping score because she was no longer interested in saving their relationship. My Father had never kept score because he wanted nothing more than to cultivate a relationship with me. He had done that, not by throwing my scorecard away, but by completely filling it out himself.

That's what Paul meant when he said that Jesus died on the cross so that, "the righteous requirements of the law might be fully met in us, who do not live according to the sinful nature but according to the Spirit" (Rom. 8:4). For someone who had lived many years imagining God as the divine Scorekeeper, this moment was an epiphany.

God's not counting anymore, and that means I don't have to either!

NOT LESS-LOVED BUT FULLY-LOVED

If Adam and Eve's troubles began when they lost sight of how deeply God loved them, doesn't it stand to reason that our whole lives will change when we come to know the depth of his love for us? That's exactly what our Father wants the reality of the cross to produce in us.

In this final section, we will look at what it means to live every day in the confidence of his love for us. We'll discover that when living in this reality everything about our life and our faith will take on different meaning and tap new motivations. Rather than providing an excuse for falling victim to sin, our security in his love will actually destroy the root of sin and teach us how to live as his free people in the earth.

But let us be certain of the process at the outset. You cannot implement the practical implications as an attempt to become secure in his love. That is backwards; confusing the cause with the results. It will only produce another form of legalism—trying to earn by effort what God has made a gift.

Freedom to grow in him comes when you recognize that his love for you isn't affected by your actions. Philip Yancey in his book, *What's So Amazing About Grace?*, said it as clearly as we need to understand it: "Grace means there is nothing we can do to make God love us more... and there is nothing we can do to make God love us less. God already loves us as much as an infinite God can possibly love."

Our only choice is whether or not to *live* loved; trusting that his eye is on us and that he can work out in us everything that he desires. That is the challenge of life in God's kingdom. He has done everything to demonstrate is irrefutable love; but he will not make us live there. We can still live less-loved, pursing our own agenda with our own resources and in the process not only destroying ourselves but hurting others as well.

The choice is yours; and it can never be made once for a lifetime. This choice is made every day in every circumstance in which you find yourself. Do you trust that he loves you even in this, or will you fall back on your own wisdom and desires?

NOT RELIGION, BUT RELATIONSHIP

There are two ways to hide from God's love—rebellion and religion. Rebellion, illustrated in the prodigal son, defies God's love and seeks to cover up guilt and shame through the indulgence of sensual desires. Religion, on the other hand, is far more subtle. It seeks its cover-up with good works and obligation. However, like the prodigal's older brother, it still denies the Father's place in our lives and leads us no closer to knowing him for who he really is.

Simply, religion is keeping score—striving for acceptance through our own performance whether it be in our good works or some ritualistic exercise. Those things squarely put the focus on us and what we can do to be accepted by God and all these are doomed to fail.

Most of Paul's letters were written because even the earliest believers found themselves trading relationship for religion. Instead of learning to live in the security of his love they would go back to the traditions, creeds, disciplines and laws as an attempt to earn it themselves. He reminded them over and over again, that God's love would take them further than their own efforts and achievements ever would. But his words often fell on deaf ears then, as they have in generations since.

Why do so many enjoy striving for God's acceptance, even after he went to such lengths to prove it was already ours? Perhaps people feel more secure if they can control the relationship. Perhaps they're afraid that if they no longer have to earn his acceptance they'll find themselves using grace as an excuse to pursue their selfish desires. Perhaps they don't want a relationship with him at all, simply his help in time of need and that coveted "Get-Out-Of-Hell-Free Card."

Religion offers us the illusion of earning acceptance, but it is only a cheap substitute for the reality of life in him. God's desire is to engage us in a life-changing relationship. He knew the 'life-changing' would come only out of the relationship, thus he demonstrated his love for us before we did anything to make ourselves worthy of it. By doing so, he wanted us to stop trying to earn it and just live in light of it.

What would you do today if you knew God absolutely loved you? God knows the answer to that question will lead you further into his life than the strivings of religion ever can. The key to living a productive Christian life is not waking up everyday trying to be loved by God, but waking up in the awareness that you are already his beloved.

NOT A FORMULA, BUT A FRIENDSHIP

By releasing us from the terrible burden of trying to earn his friendship God put the focus right where he wanted it—on the relationship he always wanted to have with each of us. He wants to be a closer friend than any other we've ever had: sharing our joys, our pains, even our failures as he teaches us how to live in him.

Daily, God wants us to discover more about him and how he wants to be involved with us. This is an intensely personal process. Try as we might to standardize that relationship by offering a checklist as to how to cultivate it; we will always fall short. No living relationship thrives through the use of a checklist, because they are far more dynamic than any list can facilitate. God can be personal enough to develop this friendship with each of us as we invite him to do so.

Some people have asked me if this kind of friendship risks trivializing God and reduces our awe of him. I have not found that to be so. Those who treat God as a buddy who thinks and acts just like they do, always make me wonder if it's the Living God they've found or is it an illusion of their own mind? God is who he is. He is the Almighty, Holy God who created the heavens and the earth. He is more magnificent than we can ever conceive. I can only approach him with confidence because that's the way he wanted it, but that doesn't diminish in my mind for one moment who he is.

Some have argued that if we wouldn't be so casual with an earthly sovereign, why would we presume to do so with God Almighty. I know what they mean. If I had the opportunity to meet a president or king I would dress up in my finest and extend him all the decorum his station demanded. But it would be impossible to become his friend in that environment, wouldn't it?

Does the king or president want that with everyone? I wouldn't think so. Who can go to the president in their comfortable clothes, jump up on his lap and laugh and play with him? His children, of course. That's what God has offered us, not the relationship of a subject but that of a son or daughter who can know him as he really is and not be intimidated by that. He didn't want to use his magnificence to dwarf us, but to elevate us into a friendship with an incredible Father. That could never make him less awesome, only more so.

NOT FOR HIM, BUT WITH HIM

As you grow increasingly certain that his love for you is not connected to your performance you will find yourself released from the horrible burden of doing something for him. You'll realize that your greatest ideas and most passionate deeds will fall far short of what he really wants to do through you.

I used to be driven to do something great for God. I volunteered for numerous opportunities and worked hard in the hopes that some book I was writing, some church I was planting or some organization I was helping would accomplish great things for God. While I think God used my misguided zeal in spite of myself, nothing I did ever rose to the level of my expectations. Instead they seemed to distract me from God, consume my life and leave me stressed out or worn out from the pursuit.

I'm not driven anymore. I haven't tried to do anything great for God in the last four years and yet have seen him use my life in ways that always exceed my expectations. What changed? I did, by his grace.

My desire to do something great for God served me far more than it ever did him. It kept me too busy to enjoy him and distracted me from the real ministry opportunities he brought across my path every day.

I used to start my day laying out my plans before God and seeking his blessing on them. How silly! Why would I even want God to be the servant of my agenda? God's plans for my day far exceed mine. I can almost hear him now as I awaken, "Wayne, I'm going to touch some people today. Do you want to come along?"

It's amazing how gentle that is; but all the more powerful because it is. I don't have to go. God's work won't be thwarted by my lack of participation. He will touch them anyway, but I wouldn't miss it for the world. He does things I'd never dream of and uses me in ways I could never conceive. His focus on touching people instead of managing programs has revolutionized my view of ministry. It requires no less diligence on my part, but directs that diligence in far more fruitful endeavors.

If you've never known the joy of simply living in God's acceptance instead of trying to earn it, your most exciting days in Christ are ahead of you. People who learn to live out of a genuine love relationship with the God of the universe will live in more power, more joy and more righteousness than anyone motivated by fear of his judgment.

> *All this is from God, who reconciled us to himself through Christ and gave us the ministry of reconciliation: that God was reconciling the world to himself in Christ, not counting men's sins against them.*
> —2 CORINTHIANS 5:18-19

For your personal journey

Spend a few moments thinking where you are still counting in your relationship to God. Is it failures? Minutes in prayer? Number of converts? If you find yourself doing those things, ask God to help you receive what he has already given you. Stop doing anything that seeks to earn his love and learn to do what you do simply because you already have his love. This is quite a change of mind that only God's Spirit can produce.

So Sin Isn't Important to God?

*"Never let us be discouraged with ourselves; it is not when
we are conscious of our faults that we are the most wicked:
on the contrary, we are less so. We see by a brighter light.
And let us remember, for our consolation, that we never
perceive our sins till he begins to cure them."*
FRANCOIS FENELON (1651-1715)

The pastor invited me to speak to a retreat of his elders.
"Would you teach us about grace? Our leaders really need it!"

On Friday night I began to lay the foundation for an understanding of God's grace. They were not impressed. They didn't laugh at my stories or respond to my overtures. They were either suspicious of me or hostile to the material, I couldn't tell which. I hoped for better in the morning , but the mood hadn't changed at all.

After a few more moments of unsuccessfully trying to win

them over, I finally stopped. "Let me ask you a question," I began. "Am I making any sense at all?"

Eyes darted around the room uncomfortably, but most settled on an elderly gentleman in the corner. After a moment, he spoke. "What I hear you saying is that these young people coming to our church don't need to jump through the same hoops I've been forcing myself through all my life."

Good, they have got it! I thought. I nodded as he paused.

"Well, I'll tell you something." The mood got darker. "If you think I'm going to let them get away with that, you're crazy!" I glanced around the room and saw nods of agreement. Obviously I was the minority.

"So why I am I here?" I said turning to the pastor.

"I told you, we don't understand grace!"

And they didn't. Their security with God was derived from their rules and rituals and through them they had staked out the high ground above the rest of the people and were not about to give it up. They made serving God their god and missed knowing the Living God.

"BUT" THEOLOGY

I understood their dilemma, because I had lived there too. Who hasn't seen people use God's grace as an excuse to guiltlessly chase their own agenda? They accept God's forgiveness and an eternity in heaven but go on living in the same captivity as the world around them. Not wanting to apportion "cheap grace" to people who don't want to do things God's way, we find ourselves constructing a list of expectations to help define what a true Christian does.

It's as if we can only keep the message of grace intact for the first fifteen minutes of someone's birth into God's kingdom. After that we start loading them up with the obligations of being a good Christian:

"Of course we are saved by grace, *but* that doesn't mean we can just sit around and do nothing. God is a loving Father, *but* don't take advantage of that because he is also a severe judge. We are not saved by our works, *but* we still need to live a life that pleases him." The latter usually consists of some mix of Bible reading, prayer, church attendance and righteous deeds.

By embracing this "but" theology we end up right where we began, with a performance-based relationship to God. We have to live every day concerned about whether we have done enough to be a good Christian and judge others around us with the same standards. It not only takes all the joy out of knowing God, but also all the encouragement out of our relationships with others.

Whenever we add anything to God's work on the cross, the message is distorted and we rob it of its power. Paul made it clear that the cross alone had totally transformed him. "May I never boast except in the cross of our Lord Jesus Christ, through which the world has been crucified to me, and I to the world" (Gal. 6:14).

Grace doesn't need any add-ons. Even though Paul watched people who used their new-found freedom as an excuse for the flesh and warned them not to, he never sought to change them by adding human effort to grace. He knew the fix lay elsewhere.

It is as paradoxical a truth as Jesus' warning that we save our lives by losing them: living in his grace leads to freedom from sin; living in his judgment leads to even greater sin. It has always been so, though it defies human logic. That's because we are far more used to being conformed by external pressures than we are to being transformed by his inner presence. For many, having never experienced the latter, they doubt it will even work.

But it does. Once you experience God's delight over you as his child and the joy of friendship that produces, you will find yourself abandoning your own desires and embracing his. Of course that delight doesn't mean he affirms everything we do. He simply knows that without him we are powerless against sin and that no matter what strength of will we can conjure up it will only last a few months then fade into bondage again.

So God still cares about sin—deeply! Sin destroys what he loves. He wants to change you by teaching you how to live loved every day. When you learn to recognize his voice in your ear and his hand in your life, you will want to be even more like him.

THE CONSEQUENCES OF SIN

We make a fatal mistake when we try to force Scripture to offer redemption to those who only want to go to heaven, but who do not want a relationship with the Living God. By trying to offer them some minimal standard of conduct that will also allow them to qualify for salvation while continuing to pursue their own agenda, we distort the gospel, destroying its power, and concoct legalistic games to give them a false sense of security.

In fact the New Testament has nothing to say to people who want God's salvation without wanting *him*. The Scriptures are an unabashed invitation to live as a child of the most incredible Father in the universe. As you do, you will yearn to be like him. You will discover that God's way is better than anything you can imagine and you'll lay down your agenda to embrace his.

Grace doesn't mitigate all the consequences of sin. Certainly it allows God to forgive us so that our relationship with him is unimpeded by our failures and it does negate the culmination of sin in spiritual death. But, it doesn't cancel out the temporal consequences of sin.

If I vent my anger on my children, grace doesn't stop the damage it does to them, nor what it destroys in me. The person who engages in immoral behavior may still get pregnant or contract a fatal disease. If you take advantage of someone for your own gain, they still experience the loss or the pain and a murderer's victim is still dead.

Viewed this way, sin is its own punishment. I used to look at sin with longing, seeing it as a forbidden pleasure God denied us to prove our sincerity. I could look at those who seemed to get away with it in envy because I could not. But sin diminishes who God really made us to be. By putting our wisdom and desires above his it distorts who we really are and leaves a wake of hurt people behind us.

No one who understands the Father's grace will think it lets them get away with sin. Rather, it allows us to see our weaknesses and failures in the full light of God's love. It encourages us to invite the Father into the darkest places of our heart and ask him to change us.

That's why I'm suspicious of those who think repentance undoes the consequences of their sin and that people should just forgive and forget. True repentance doesn't deny the pain we've caused others, but owns up to it. Forgiveness isn't a covering for sin, but reason to be honest with our faults and seek to rectify whatever damage our sins have caused others.

GRACE WITH A PURPOSE

Those who distort grace do so because they see it only as a ticket to heaven. If the reason Jesus died on the cross was to save us from hell, then how do we get people to live the Christian life?

Such thinking misses the greater point. God did not extend his grace to us merely to forgive our sins and let us into heaven. Those are secondary benefits, not the primary objective. The purpose of grace is to grant us access into his presence every day. Grace qualifies us for the relationship we could never earn on our merits.

This grace doesn't let us get away with sin, but in fact "it teaches us how to say 'no' to ungodliness and worldly passions..." (Titus 2:12).

God knows that as we grow in friendship with him and discover how to trust the fact that he loves us completely, the root of sin will be destroyed. Grace doesn't diminish God's desire for our holiness but clarifies the process. Righteousness doesn't produce relationship. Relationship produces righteousness.

That's why Paul despised the righteousness that came from human effort. He had sampled it for most of his life. He knew it was merely an illusion of outward performance that would constantly frustrate its pursuer. Like Adam and Eve's choice to trust themselves over their Creator, it would lead him to utter failure.

But when God revealed his grace to Paul and he discovered the love that Father held in his eye for him, even after the atrocities that he had committed, Paul was changed. Knowing he deserved death and had been spared meant his life no longer belonged to him. The true treasure lies in knowing God in his fullness and the Son whom he raised from the dead.

The power of the cross had opened an eternal friendship between himself and the Father. As he learned to trust that love, Paul watched his life change. Appetites of the flesh waned and he found himself acting in ways that surprised him so much, he dared not take credit for them.

He referred to it as the righteousness that comes from trusting God and knew it was the exact opposite of the righteousness that works had produced in him. Once he tasted of the lifestyle that trust produced he never wanted to return to his old ways.

Living in the transformation that trust produces is the real deal. When you watch yourself speak a kind word where anger would have surfaced before, or find yourself uninterested in something that used to drive you mad with desire, or sacrifice something you hold dear without hardly a second thought then you will know Paul knew.

It's righteousness as only God can produce it. Taste it once and you'll never be satisfied with anything less.

> *"...that I may gain Christ and be found in him, not having a righteousness of my own that comes from the law, but that which is through faith in Christ—the righteousness that comes from God and is by faith.*
>
> —PHILIPPIANS 3:8-9

For your personal journey

Has a false notion of grace diminished your passion for righteousness, or has it made you more hungry for the righteousness that comes from trusting God? If the former, ask God to draw you closer to him so that your love for him will produce a desire to be like him. Also, look for ways that you put righteousness before relationship, thinking that your performance makes you more acceptable to God. Ask him to teach you what it means to trust you in the pressing details of your life right now.

A Lifetime of Learning to Trust

"Once God is known as Father all methods to attain to security, prosperity and assurance in the world are exposed as useless enslavement. If one knows God as Father then there is security about everything."
DAVID BOAN AND JOHN YATES
IN AN UNPUBLISHED MANUSCRIPT

The mechanic had estimated the repair to my car heater at well over $300. Imagine my shock then when I went to pick it up and he said, "That will be $18.75."

I looked at him uncertain of what I'd heard and he simply smiled back. I repeated his price in surprise. "What happened?"

"It wasn't what we thought. We found a loose connection and tightened it for you."

Being mechanically challenged and having seen too many *60 Minutes* reports on unscrupulous mechanics, I expect them all to cheat me. I've taken my car in too many times for a $30 oil change and come out with $200 of repairs I was never sure I really needed. It had never worked the other way around.

This was my first visit to that mechanic, but it certainly was not my last. By demonstrating his integrity when he could have easily taken advantage of me, he gained my trust. I went away assured that I had finally found an honest mechanic and as long as we lived in that community he was the only mechanic I allowed to touch my cars.

One simple act of integrity secured my trust in his workmanship and he's never disappointed me.

God wanted to secure our trust the same way but on a far larger scale. By taking our sin into himself and destroying it at the cost of his own life he showed us the lengths his love would go for us. That act provides a source of trust for us as constant as he is. Never again would we doubt his intentions toward us no matter what happens.

TO TRUST OR NOT TO TRUST?

Most of our lessons in trust have been incredibly painful. Haven't we all been disappointed by people we thought would treat us fairly or compassionately? Perhaps you've experienced the betrayal of people you considered close friends simply because you no longer served their needs or desires.

Through the course of life we learn to keep a wary eye on people, knowing how few trustworthy people there really are. That may sound jaded, but Jesus lived that way, too. He didn't entrust himself to anyone, because he knew what was inside people (John 2:24). So of course our attempts to trust others will often be frustrated, but that's because God never wanted us to trust others. He wanted us to love others but to trust him alone.

But learning to trust him can also be a struggle. In my spiritual journey I've often been disillusioned by trusting God. It seems so easy when all our circumstances are pleasant but when painful and desperate circumstances come crashing down on us, he sometimes seems to ignore our most ardent prayers. Who hasn't trusted God to do something then watched him seemingly fail us? How do those moments help us learn to trust?

Interestingly enough, they do! I used to think that being disillusioned with God was sinful but I have since learned it is a valuable part of the process. If I am disillusioned with God it means I had illusions about him. The fact is he has never failed to love me completely, despite how it may have appeared. He didn't do what I expected, not because he loved me less as I feared but because his way of doing things exceeds my own. "Immeasurably more than all we ask or imagine," is how Paul phrased it (Eph. 3:20).

Looking back I thought I could trust God to make my life easy, to provide what I wanted and steer me clear of any painful experiences. That wasn't God's agenda for me at all. He wanted to imprint his glory into my life; to make me a man who would bear his image to a fallen world. So he rarely dealt with circumstances the way I wanted and by not accepting the way in which he was loving me, it eroded my confidence. As long as our trust in him is based on circumstances (and our misinterpretation of them) it will shift as often as the winds.

Through the cross God provided a way for us to trust him that would transcend our own preferences and intellect, a way that is able to take us through the darkest circumstances not doubting his love, but resting in it.

LEARNING THE LANGUAGE OF GOD

A year ago I traveled around France for a month while on a speaking tour. Often I stayed in homes where no one was able to speak English. I found it frustrating to live so near some of God's treasures without the language to hear their stories.

I have felt like that too in my journey with God. Often I have no idea what he's trying to say to me, or what he's trying to do in my life. I am more comfortable with the language of human effort and anxiety than I am the language of trust. But this is one treasure I'm not going to miss no matter how hard it is for me to learn.

Trusting the Father's love for you simply means that every day, in every circumstance you can rest assured God knows who you are, cares more deeply about you than you do yourself and is capable of working out his glory in you.

When you trust him you will find yourself cooperating with his work going on in you and around you. Trust is not coasting through life assuming that whatever happens must be God. Rather it is an active partnership that rises out of your relationship to him. Without that what many call trust is simply a Christian version of fatalism or complacency.

Whenever I talk about trust the question invariably arises: "Does that mean I just do nothing and God will do it all?" We are so schooled in trusting our own efforts that we can't see anything beyond that. We equate trusting him with doing nothing because we know that most of what we do is driven by the fact that we don't think he's doing anything at all.

Trusting God doesn't lead to lethargy nor does it provide an excuse to be slothful. Those who are learning to trust God will discover how to actively participate with him in the work he is doing. Even though Paul warned us against trusting our own efforts, he showed us that cooperating with him can be costly. "To this end I labor, struggling with all his energy, which so powerfully works in me" (Col. 1:29).

The difference is striking. For many years I thought I knew what God wanted with my life and pursued it with a passion. Others encouraged me, thinking it was what God wanted too.

Most of that agenda, however, was motivated by my own insecurities and need to be successful. No matter how I dressed that up by calling it God's promise, or thinking that my success would benefit the kingdom of God, he did not help me pursue my own agenda.

Trying to make it happen on my own led to frustration and burn-out. As I've grown to trust him more and see more clearly what he wants to accomplish in and through my life, I find myself even more willing to go the extra mile in what he asks me to do. When I'm on his agenda, I find, like Paul, that it taps a deeper reserve than mere human effort. It allows me to draw from his strength that does not burn us out.

When Jesus asked people to "repent and believe" the gospel, he was not asking them to be sorry for their sins and embrace an orthodox theology. He was asking them to forfeit their own agenda and embrace his. That's the invitation to the kingdom. It is not whether we want to go to heaven or hell but whether we want to trust God or continue trusting ourselves.

To do that he will teach us how to recognize his presence with us. He will teach us how to understand his heart and how to confidently follow his will. But the curriculum for that is not where you might first expect it.

LIFE AT THE END OF YOUR ROPE

Jesus seemed to think backwards about everything. "You are blessed when you're at the end of your rope. With less of you there is more of God and his rule." That's how Eugene Peterson translates the first beatitude in *The Message* and I think he gets to the heart of it.

I've never heard anyone stand up during testimony time and say, "I know I'm really blessed today because I'm all out of options. I've lost everything and am at the end of my rope with nothing left to hold on to." We don't think such people blessed. We think them needy. We consider ourselves blessed when all our needs are met and there are no dark clouds on the horizon. But we are wrong.

Every New Testament writer echoes Jesus' words. All of them tell us that we can rejoice in our most difficult moments because Jesus will be working things out in those seasons that we would never let him touch when all is well. He didn't tell us to rejoice for the bad times; but *in them* because he would convert our pain into his glory.

The truth is we only grow in trust at moments of extremity. If we can do it ourselves, we will! If we're sure we can fix things we won't listen for him. If we have enough money, time, energy, talent, or know others who do, we'll try that first.

Taking us to the end of our rope is really taking us to the end of ourselves. That's why he calls us blessed at those moments. While I appreciate the seasons of rest and refreshing he brings into my life, I realize that only by facing my own inadequacies and the foolishness of my own desires can I really experience the glory of God's kingdom. We don't come easily to those moments, but when we finally give up trying to save ourselves, that's where we taste of his immeasurable glory.

Along this journey you will notice that every good thing he has imprinted in your heart came at your most difficult moments. I don't think for a moment that God orchestrates these times because the consequences of living in a fallen world will provide ample opportunities. What amazes me is how he uses the most hurtful moments for his purpose. You'll even see him use what others intend for evil to purify your heart and teach you to depend on him even more.

Much of the curriculum for this journey lies in the very circumstances you're begging God to change. This journey is at once more painful than you can imagine and also, filled with more wonder than you can contain. Don't think it a broad road for it is not. You'll find even your dearest friends in Christ may not understand the most difficult places in your journey. But trust him to take you through them and he will. In doing so he will make you a little more like him.

I don't know that we'll ever get comfortable at the end of the rope, but at least we don't have to dread it or think he has abandoned us.

BEYOND YOUR FAILURES

A friend of mine recently lost his job and is actively seeking another. One morning he told me that a plum job just escaped his grasp and that someone far less qualified than him got it.

Knowing my friend's desire to live in God's life, I asked him if he thought anything could have prevented him from getting that job if God wanted it for him. "If I messed up, somehow," he responded.

"So are you saying that God isn't bigger than your mistakes?"

It's a misconception far too many of us indulge. If our freedom to trust God hinges on our ability to get everything right then we're really back to trusting ourselves, aren't we? If God isn't bigger than my halting attempts to learn how to walk with him, I might as well give up now.

But he is! That's the lesson he taught Peter on the night he let him face the biggest failure of his life. He told him it would happen, but Peter was certain that he was strong enough to endure any threat to his relationship with Jesus.

Don't you wish Jesus had just sent Peter home, telling him to lock the doors, crawl under the covers and wait for Sunday morning? Jesus didn't even try to stop Peter from following him to Caiaphas' house where he would betray his friend.

What's even more amazing is that before Peter even messes up, Jesus already prayed him past it. "But I have prayed for you, that your faith may not fail. And when you have turned back, strengthen your brothers"(Luke 2:32). Please understand what Jesus was doing here. He had already factored Peter's failure in before he had made it. He knew what Peter didn't know. He could have saved him the anguish, but he wanted Peter to come to the end of his rope and learn that he could not trust in his own ability to follow Jesus.

I suspect it was the most painful but most joyous lesson Peter ever learned. Where there was less of Peter, there was more of God and his rule. Don't think for a moment that the slips and spills of learning to live in the Father's love will exclude you from his table. God is able to work in you and through you despite what you lack.

He knows that learning to live in the confidence of his love amidst the realities of everyday life is the most difficult thing you'll ever learn.

A JOURNEY FOR A LIFETIME

One of my friends had been shackled by perfectionism. Whenever we talked about grace, he wanted to believe it, but was always so aware of his shortcomings that he couldn't bring himself to trust God until he performed better.

But one day God used a hobby of his to teach him about grace. He loves to work with wood and to make decorations for his home. The light dawned for him when he noticed how differently he and his wife view his hobby. She loves the finished product and delights in displaying it in their home. He, however, enjoys the process of making it far more. He loves to take a raw piece of wood and fashion it. Once it's finished he is already on to what he wants to do next. "I finally realized that God not only wants the product, but he actually enjoys the process."

He's right. God enjoys taking fearful slaves to sin and teaching them how to live as beloved sons and daughters. He knows how to peel off layers of selfishness and shame to shape his image in us.

That's why the writer of Hebrews called Jesus the Author and Finisher of our faith. He initiated it on the cross and with painstaking care he continues to carve, sand and buff until we become the treasure he fashioned in his heart at the beginning of time.

It's a process he controls from start to finish, and it's a journey that will last a lifetime. You can't make it happen, but you can choose to trust him and watch the incredible process he'll use to produce his glory in you.

> *If God is for us, who can be against us? He who did not spare his own Son, but gave him up for us all how will he not also, along with him, graciously give us all things?*
> —ROMANS 8:31-32

For your personal journey

Where are you being stretched to the end of your rope? Where is God exposing the weaknesses of your own strength and the foolishness of your best wisdom? Give up the idea that your failures have brought you to this moment for it is an incredible work of God calling you to trust him more than you have in the past. Ask God to teach you how to give up self-sufficiency and learn to trust him. Then do whatever it is that trusting God's love would lead you to do and learn to ignore the ravings of your anxieties and fears.

Shamelessly Free

"(When you) become totally dependent upon the life of Christ... (you will never be) so released at last from the self distrust which has made you at one moment an arrogant loud-mouthed braggart, and the next moment the victim of your own self-pity—and either way, always in bondage to the fear of other men's opinions."

MAJOR IAN THOMAS IN *THE SAVING LIFE OF CHRIST*

She can wear many disguises so well it's not always easy to recognize her.

She will help you boast at your achievements and contrive excuses for your mistakes.

She can turn a simple gift of God into feelings of superiority; and then at the first sign of trouble plunge you to the depths of inferiority.

She can take you captive through the compliments of others

and make you feel rejected by the most genuine criticism.

She can make you rabidly chase an illusion of success that never satisfies and completely paralyze you with a fear of failure.

She will let you take credit for good things you don't deserve and blame others for their hard times.

One minute she can make you smug in self-righteousness and the next overwhelm you with guilt and self-loathing.

Shame is the unfortunate inheritance of humanities captivity in sin. You were born with her whispering in your ear. Until you find freedom from her in the Father's love she will, like a spreading cancer, sink her tentacles into everything you think or do.

What a horrible burden it is to measure our worth by everything we do and every word spoken about us. As long as you listen to her she will devour your energy and leave you with a distorted perspective of God's work in you and those around you. Since the day Adam covered up for her with those itchy fig leaves, we are at our worst when following her counsel or trying to hide her presence.

But when you find your security in the awesome love of God, her voice is unmasked. No longer do you have to play her games by worrying about what others think. Then you'll really know what it is to live as God's child in the earth.

A TOUCHDOWN FOR JESUS

He was a high-priced cornerback playing for a professional football team, and suffering from an overdose of media scrutiny. Having sold his talents as a free agent, his subsequent performance had been disappointing. People were saying he was overpriced and overrated. Twice that evening he had been beaten for touchdowns and knew the media would have a field day with his performance. But a few minutes into overtime he intercepted a pass and ran it back for the winning touchdown.

As the Monday night telecast went off the air, they shoved a microphone into the celebration. Through an irrepressible, mile-wide grin he yelled, "I just thank the Lord Jesus for giving me the chance to prove myself. I felt like he was saying that I had the faith to make this happen."

While he celebrated his touchdown, I grieved for his theology. He unmasked his own shame by boasting that his touchdown validated his faith. Can you imagine what he lives with every day, if he links his trust in God to his performance on a football field?

I cringe when most professional athletes talk about God. What comes out often paints God as a success deity, rewarding the faithful with victory. One of those I respect the most said his Super Bowl victory vindicated his obedience to play for a certain team. What about the men God had called to the city who lost the Super Bowl? Was their obedience less significant or their lives less valuable to God?

Other athletes have said that God rewards those with victories who will give him the most glory. Is that why we see people kneel down in the end zone and acknowledge God after a touchdown, but get angry when they miss a tackle or throw an interception?

You can't blame them, really. To get to the highest echelon of athletic competition, these men and women have learned to live on the success of their performance. They've been trained to measure their value by it because that's how everyone else around them measures it. They've obviously had a lot of success to get to that level of competition. But it can result in some greatly distorted values.

Watch a championship game or a match and you'll notice that the highs of winning are just too high; and the lows are too low. Rather than championships perhaps they could be called pageants to manic-depressiveness. No moderate ground exists here. John Madden, the Fox Sports analyst said of professional sports that the "The highs of winning never equal the lows of losing." Even coming out second best in all the world seemingly forces them to slink off in shame and suffer months of embarrassment. Even fans take on the same attitudes of superiority or shame.

Please don't read this as an indictment against professional athletes, because we all do it. It's just that most of our best or our worst moments aren't on television.

SHAME-BASED LIVING

We have all felt the pervasive power of shame when we've been embarrassed by something we've done or something someone else has said. Our face flushes and stomach grinds, and we want to dig a hole and crawl into it. But it also works much deeper than that.

Shame tells us that no one could possibly love us if they really knew what we had been part of in the past or knew the temptations, doubts and motives that still lurk beneath the surface. Don't you have things you hope no one else ever finds out about you?

So we pretend to be whatever we think will make us feel included and don't realize that everyone else is doing it too. Almost every time someone asks for my help to deal with a sin or struggle they almost always preface their confession with a disclaimer. "I know probably no one else is dealing with this, but..." Shame often keeps us from being authentic enough to realize that others are struggling with the same things we are.

Feeling inferior is only one side of shame. Those who act superior and those who boast in their accomplishments also are reacting to shame. Those behaviors only act as a cover for a deep sense of personal inadequacy, usually at other people's expense.

All of this shame makes us easy to manipulate. Our desire to be liked, to fit in, and not be embarrassed are what the world uses to press us into its mold and what we often use to get what we want from others. Most advertising appeals to these motives at some level.

Organized religion can also be a master of its use. When people want us to do something for them, they will press on these self-needs as a way to make us respond. Shame makes it impossible for us to say no and gives power to gossip. It threatens us with humiliation or of being left if we don't conform to what others want and it promises approval and affirmation when we do.

We learn this pattern early. Children are often made to feel that they are loved and appreciated to the degree that they can meet their parents' expectations. It's ironic then that parents are so mystified about the effects of peer pressure when their children start caring more about what their friends think of them than what their parents do. It's the same use of shame.

The fear of "what others might think" can both restrain us from doing what we know is right and entice us to do what ultimately harms us.

I remember receiving a gold-plated pin when I was eleven years old for two years of unbroken attendance at Sunday School. The affirmation I received for my accomplishment and the applause of all the adults in the congregation was an intoxicating brew. It made me feel superior to others who had not been so dedicated and helped launch me on a persistent quest to drink of that well for most of my spiritual journey.

I thought that thirst was my friend beckoning me closer to Jesus, not realizing for almost thirty years it was my jailer, pushing me to serve other people's expectations. Jesus didn't want to use my shame to spur me to greater things but to set me free from it.

SHAME-FREE LIVING

The story has always amazed me. A woman whose reputation for sin was well known in her community, walked into the home of a Pharisee as a group of them were sharing a meal with Jesus. She made her way around the table until she found him, then poured expensive perfume over his feet and wiped them with her hair.

How could she even go into a home of those who despised her so much? And how could she touch Jesus that way when surely everyone in the room would misinterpret her act of love? Shouldn't she have been too ashamed to even show her face there? You would think so, but no! Obviously she had been deeply touched by Jesus, her sins had been forgiven and now the only thing that mattered to her in that roomful of disparaging looks was the look of appreciation she saw in his eyes.

What began in the Garden—our utter sense of shame—is swallowed up in the presence of Jesus. She was liberated from the oppressive need of worrying about what others thought of her and was able to simply do what she wanted to do most. Discovering how much the Father loves will increasingly set you free to walk without shame, before God and with other people. Though shame restrains people from sin under the law, in Christ it no longer holds any purpose.

Because your sin was consumed in Jesus on the cross, there is absolutely no condemnation or guilt for anyone who lives in him. You can taste this miracle of the cross every day. Now you can be with your Father just like you are, still in the process of transformation, and not have to hide anything. You can share with him your darkest secrets as you learn from him how to walk free of it. He knows you cannot fix it yourself and only awaits for you to recognize it and invite his help.

As he teaches you how to walk shamelessly with him, you'll also discover yourself walking shamelessly in the world. Having been bullied by shame all of your life, often without even recognizing it, you will be amazed at how much your life will change in its absence

It's an incredible gift that Dallas Willard in *The Divine Conspiracy* painted this way: "Would you like to have no need for others to praise you, and would you like not to be paralyzed and humiliated by their dislike and condemnation? Wouldn't you also like to have a strength and understanding that enables you genuinely and naturally to bless those who are cursing you—or cheating you, beating you out on the job, spitting on you in a confrontation, laughing at your religion or culture, even killing you?"

Those who are no longer influenced by shame can finally live authentic lives—the same outside as they are inside. It is a tremendous relief to be known exactly for who you are, allowing people to know both your strengths and your weaknesses. Shame-free people champion reality over image, sincerity over pretentiousness and honesty over deceit. Admittedly there is a cost to living authentically in a broken world as others try to take advantage of you. But no one I've met who had done so would go back to the land of pretense.

OF NO REPUTATION

I have been a slave to my reputation almost my entire life and it has been an oppressive burden. I first saw it weakening in my life in a conversation with a friend. She had asked me to write her a letter explaining my role in mediating a dispute between her and her business partner. They had begun the business out of their close friendship and now they could no longer work together. They couldn't agree on how to split up the business and asked for my help. I told them at the outset we probably couldn't find a resolution they both thought fair, but could perhaps find one where they both felt equally cheated. A few hours of piecing together various options finally brought a solution.

Now, some six months later, one of them was calling me saying that the other was telling her friends how she had been cheated out of the business. She wanted me to write a letter describing the process we had been through to prove her a liar.

"I am willing to do that, Jill," I said on the phone, "but let me give you something to consider first. This may be an opportunity for you to die to your reputation." As the words came out of my mouth I remember cocking my head in surprise that I had said them.

For the previous four years I had also been the victim of some rumors spread about me and my family by those who wanted to discredit my ministry. I had often prepared responses to the lies that were being told, but each time God had prevented me from mailing them. "I want you to give up serving your reputation and trust it to me," was all he would tell me. I remembered that Jesus made himself of no reputation. It was the most painful season of my life. How could I encourage anyone toward a similar process?

But that morning it dawned on me how much the past four years had worked the Father's freedom into my life. If people misunderstood my ministry or believed lies about me, that was God's business not mine. Mine was to simply do what he asked without the horrible need to defend myself and make sure other people liked me in the process. Now I could enjoy the fruits of his freedom.

I wanted Jill to have the same thing, though she was shocked by my offer. I told her my story and finished with these words, "Jill, as long as you have to guard your reputation you are the slave of anyone who chooses to lie about you. Those who know you well enough won't need a letter; and those who don't, won't believe it anyway."

I never wrote the letter and Jill got to discover the incredible joy of living free of other people's opinions. I know it was painful, but when you know the Father loves you completely and that your reputation is secure in his hands, you will never again have to appeal for the approval of others.

That freedom will not only be one of the greatest blessings of the journey, but it is also the key to loving other people the way you've been loved yourself.

> *To him who is able to keep you from falling and to present you before his glorious presence without fault and with great joy—to the only God our Savior be glory, majesty, power and authority, through Jesus Christ our Lord.*
>
> —JUDE 24-25

For your personal journey

Ask God how shame-based behaviors are manifesting themselves in your relationship with him. Look for him to identify where boasting, blaming, gossip, self-pity, and worrying about what others think are causing you to live to shame instead of living to him. Also ask him to reveal to you all the places where covering up for shame hurts your relationships with others. Ask God to draw you close enough to him so that you will no longer need to live in bondage to shame.

In Exactly
the Same Way

*"Grace does not exist to make us successful. God's grace
exists to point people to a love like no other love they have
ever known. A love outside the lines."*
MIKE YACONELLI IN *DANGEROUS WONDER*

He didn't keep it to himself. It might have been impossible—
even for God! To hold something so beautiful for himself was
unthinkable.

He had enjoyed it forever in the divine relationship of
Father, Son and Spirit. He wanted to share it so much that he
made a universe to house those he would create to be its object.

Genuine love is like that. Part of reveling in its delights is to
share it with others. When you really touch it, just try and contain
it if you can. If God didn't, how do you think you'll pull it off?

The earliest believers transformed by the cross couldn't, even
when they were being beaten with whips or battered with

stones. When they were commanded to silence they responded, "We cannot help speaking about what we have seen and heard" (Acts 4:20).

They had been touched by the greatest force in the universe and they were unable to keep it in, even when they knew it would cost them dearly. Such is the nature of God's love. As I said at the outset, there is nothing more powerful in all the world and once you've experienced God's kind of love, there will be no way for you to keep it to yourself.

THE WELLSPRING OF LOVE

I'll have to admit that I grew up viewing love as an onerous chore. Loving others meant I had to be nice to them, even when I didn't want to. Lacking compassion, I still thought I had to act compassionately at least toward other believers.

Trying to share God's love with the world was a bit more confusing and often embarrassing. We knew we were supposed to share the gospel with them, but often we talked about them as enemies meriting God's judgment. Most attempts to share God's love were driven by our feeling condemned if we didn't.

Because our motives lay more with our needs than theirs, we weren't really loving them. That was probably more obvious to them than it was to us. Instead of feeling loved, they felt exploited by those who want to get another notch on their belts.

Jesus didn't call us to convert the world, but to love others the way we've been loved. As long as we act out of obligation toward others we will fall far short. But he also knows that we cannot love effectively if we have not been loved extravagantly. That may seem selfish, but until we trust our Father to care for us, we will constantly use the people around us to meet our needs.

The unfolding of love in our lives can only begin with the wellspring of love, the Father himself! "This is love: not that we loved God, but that he loved us and sent his Son as an atoning sacrifice for our sins" (1 John 4:10). Once we experience love as God defines it we will not be able to keep from sharing it with others as it has been shared with us.

Where God is generous with you, you can be generous with others. Where God affirms your worth in him, you won't seek its substitute with others. Where you know God overlooks your flaws; you'll overlook them in others.

Jesus left us with one command: to love one another as we have been loved. Paul even placed love on a higher plane than spiritual knowledge, noting that knowledge can easily puff us up whereas love will build up others (1 Cor. 8:1). He thought it absurd that believers would trample those for whom Christ died over disputes about what foods to eat or days to celebrate. But it happened in his day and through the course of history because we've made Christianity more about doctrine than love.

HEALTHY RELATIONSHIPS

You will soon find that your security in God's love and your awareness of his unlimited patience with you will redefine the other relationships in your life.

Instead of demanding that others conform to what you think is right, you will find yourself letting others have their own journey. By no longer manipulating them to what you think is best you can allow them the same freedom God gives you. You will let them choose their own course based on nothing but the clarity of truth as they understand it and the willingness of their conscience. It is the task of the Holy Spirit to convict, not yours.

Instead of despising people who are broken by sin you will be touched by the depth of bondage that holds them captive. You will also see better how the Father is responding to them better and then know how you can. Sometimes that means you'll stand back and let the consequences of sin take their course as the father did with his prodigal son. At other times it means you'll jump into the mess with them and help them find God's way out.

Instead of saying what you think people want to hear, you'll look for ways to be gently honest with them. Human love seeks people's comfort at the expense of truth. God's love seeks people's comfort in the midst of truth. He doesn't avoid the difficult moment or hold his peace just to be nice. As you experience that in your own relationship with him you'll find yourself unable to be disingenuous with people.

Finally, by looking to God as the resource for your needs you will find yourself not overloading your friendships with expectations that are easily disappointed. By vesting all of our hope in God's ability to meet our needs we will not need to force our friends to do it. I know God will often use other believers to extend his gifts and graces to me, but now I also know I don't get to choose the vessel he uses. In other words, I always look for how God is revealing himself to me through other believers, but I don't trick myself into thinking it has to come from a specific person I want him to use.

Disappointed expectations destroy relationships because we look to others in ways God wants us to look to him. Such expectations set us up for enduring frustration. However, when we give up our expectations of people, we'll find God using some of the most unlikely people to lend us a hand. Our frustration will yield to gratefulness at however, whenever and through whomever God uses others to touch us or us to touch others.

A SAFE HARBOR

Instead of trying to fix people in crisis, love will call us to graciously lend them our support. We will be able to offer insights as fellow-strugglers in the process, not experts with pat answers. When you live like that you will be a safe place for people to be encouraged in their trials and for them to discover what it means to rely on God in the midst of it.

People who serve the illusion of a demanding God will be unwittingly destructive to people in pain instead of helpful. When I thought I had to work so hard to earn God's acceptance, I thought loving people meant I had to push them to do so as well. When someone came to me in crisis, I would tell them what they were doing wrong and encourage them to try harder. No wonder people in pain shied away from me.

I discovered that a few years ago as I was sitting in a roomful of people going through some very painful life experiences: lost jobs; family crisis, desperately ill relatives; chronic diseases, and drug dependencies. Thinking out loud I observed that it seemed to be a tough time for God's people. A few years ago, I noted, that most believers I knew were living the bliss of the American dream—stable families, healthy children, rising incomes.

Knowing glances shot around the room. "Should we tell him?" someone finally asked.

"Tell me what?"

"Back then you were not a safe person for people who were hurting. You had an answer for everything and it usually added to people's feelings of condemnation and inadequacy. But the difficulties you experienced in the last few years have changed you. People sense your compassion and your trust that the Father will sort it out with them in his time."

If all the pain I've gone through opens that door for others, I can truly say it has been worth it. But again, this is nothing I set out to change. Somehow some of the patience God had poured into me had splashed out on to others without my notice.

I am amazed at what love will call people to do, and they won't even think it a sacrifice. Recently I met a woman from the Midwest who had been divorced when her husband told her he was gay, that he had AIDS and that he wanted to live with his lover. A few years later as the disease progressed, she felt compassion for her former husband and felt God wanted her to help care for him as the disease worsened.

She did just that. With her husband's permission she moved back in, not as wife but as nurse, and cared for him as the disease progressed. I can't imagine what it took for her to give of herself in this way, and don't think her obedience should become a standard for others, but she talked about it as one of the greatest experiences of her life. What's more, after his death she took in other AIDS patients for the next few years to share God's love with them as well.

THE EXCELLENT WAY

Without God's love filling our hearts, we'll end up hurting people despite our best intentions. For years I've heard of congregations doing "Jericho marches" around property they needed to expand their facility to reach their neighborhood more effectively for the kingdom. I heard one pastor telling how one of their next-door neighbors sold them the property they needed after they went out on a Sunday evening and marched around it singing and praying that the owners would sell.

A few years later I got a look from the other side of those curtains. Our new neighbors were not Christians and let us know in no uncertain terms that they didn't want that "Jesus stuff crammed down their throats." We assured them we would not. As we got to know them better we found out why. Their previous home had been located next to a church facility and according to them the people there had been obnoxious in their attempts to make them move. They parked in their driveway, trampled their flowers, and even one night marched around the house chanting. As an elderly couple it had scared them half to death.

They had held their ground for many years thereafter unwilling to give in. When they finally did move they were embittered at how they had been treated and had rejected any sense of God's reality.

Over the course of the next thirteen years, however, we got to know them, mostly by taking them their mail when it had mistakenly ended up in our box. They mentioned one day how much they appreciated some article I'd written for the local paper and our conversations more frequently turned to spiritual things. They were interested but still cautious.

Do you know what finally opened the door? One day I found out they were too ill to get their paper any more and had to wait until the evening when their son would come over and get it for them. I told them I'd be happy to get theirs every morning when I got mine. For the next four years, until we moved, it was our family project. It wasn't any big deal to us and yet it touched them deeply.

I did get to share the life of Jesus with them and was even asked to preside at the husband's funeral when he passed away a couple of years ago. They were not "missionary projects" to us, they were friends and neighbors whom we cared about.

God's kind of love is really the most powerful force in the universe. No wonder Paul said that to really love like God loves will fulfill every bit of the law without even trying. Jesus said the same thing. "If anyone loves me, he will obey my teaching" (John 14:23).

I know that can be taken two ways and for most of my life I've followed the wrong one. I thought Jesus was saying if I really loved him I would keep all of his commands, as if the keeping was proof of the loving. But the rest of his actions and teaching prove otherwise. Those who love will find themselves obeying his ways. The keeping is the natural result of the loving.

The difference is critical, for it determines where we'll invest our efforts—in keeping or loving. We know our best efforts at keeping will never be enough but the transformation that love brings to our lives will help us live like Jesus in the world.

That's why he told us to love—exactly the same way he loves us. Until we know he does, we can't.

Once we fully know he does, we can't help ourselves not to.

This is love: not that we loved God, but that he loved us and sent his Son as an atoning sacrifice for our sins.
—1 JOHN 4:10

For your personal journey

Realize that loving others is the overflow of being loved. Wherever you see your life being given away to help others, rejoice at what God has worked in you. Wherever you see your love lacking toward others, ask God to take you to deeper levels of his love. Let him show you where you have expectations of others that prevent you from loving them freely and let him set you free.

22

The Prayer God Always Answers

"Since God offers to manage our affairs for us, let us once and for all hand them over to His infinite wisdom, in order to occupy ourselves only with Himself and what belongs to Him."
J. P. DE CAUSSADE (C. 1700S)

His time of teaching about his Father's kingdom had drawn to an end. There would be no more opportunity to hold a leper in his hands or sit in Mary's home in Bethany and talk of his Father's wonders, at least not in this body, not in the way he had grown accustomed.

He had returned to Jerusalem for his final visit. Days away from yielding himself to those who sought to kill him, his heart was deeply troubled. He stood on the threshold of the greatest act of love and trust our world would ever behold, but he knew in doing so he would be consumed.

What should he do? Would he trust his Father's love and continue the journey, or would he cut it short in a moment of weakness and beckon angels to set him free?

Perhaps the most powerful lesson he taught his disciples about prayer began by polling how they thought he should pray: "What shall I say? 'Father, save me from this hour?'"

Perhaps there were nods around the circle as they all acknowledged how good that sounded to them. That's how we're used to praying. In moments of trial and pain, it is natural even for the unbeliever to cry out for help. Save me, God! If you get me out of this I will serve you forever.

His disciples understood that prayer well enough, but Jesus wanted them to learn a better way. Even when it was his life at stake, Jesus was tuned to a better frequency. "No, it was for this very reason I came to this hour." What he wanted personally wasn't in the picture. He was focused elsewhere—on the purpose that transcended his personal happiness.

Then he prayed the prayer he wanted them to hear, "Father, glorify your name" (John 12:27).

In this brief exchange we learn everything we will need to know about prayer and what it means to follow God in this life. For every situation you'll ever encounter will offer you two options in prayer: "Father, save me" or "Father, glorify your name!"

One will lead you to frustration and disillusionment; the other to the greatest wonders in God's heart.

WHATEVER YOU ASK?

Jesus teaching about prayer seemed to be incredibly simple: Ask for whatever they wish and be assured that the Father will give it to you.

It only gets complicated when our experience with prayer falls short of this ideal. Why would he tantalize us with such outlandish promises only to leave us disappointed in so many of the things we ask?

It's not so difficult to understand why he would ignore our more selfish requests. Even his disciples had to learn that the power of prayer was not for their selfish agendas. Instead of calling down fire from heaven as James and John had asked for; Jesus taught them that such ideas came from the wrong place. And when they asked him to grant them seats on his right and left in heaven; he told them they weren't his to give and that in his Father's house there is no place for anyone to set themselves over anyone else.

Jesus never intended prayer to be the way we manipulate God to do what we think is best. If you look carefully at Jesus' simple statements about prayer you will see that they are set in the midst of us participating in what God is doing. While we are invited to make any request of God we like, the prayers that move God's hand are those that grow out of our trust in who he is and what he is doing.

I wonder what my life would be like now if God had given me half the things for which I've asked him. I know I would have been giddy with delight in the short-term, but I would have had no idea of the hurt my selfish requests would have caused. And how would I have come to know him as my loving Father if I treated him like my genie in a bottle?

It's far more difficult to understand why our prayers for other people in pain and misery go unanswered. Was Peter responding in any way less than love when he forbid Jesus to go to Jerusalem to face his executioners? I think not. Yet his entreaty was met with the harshest rebuke, as Satan's words to keep Jesus from his mission.

Peter didn't understand God's higher purpose in the cross Jesus would suffer. For God to have answered his prayer he would have aborted the very act that would save Peter from himself. "You do not have in mind the things of God, but the things of men" (Matt. 16:23) Because Peter didn't understand that his concern simply gave voice to Satan's attempt to discourage Jesus in his obedience to his Father.

It was a "save me" prayer, rising more out of fear than God's love and like most "save me" prayers, they usually resist God's purpose rather than serve it.

"FATHER, GLORIFY YOUR NAME"

We were made for this!

When God fashioned the first humans he designed them body, mind and soul so they could participate in the his glory and share in his pleasure.

If you've ever known that glory, either just sitting in his presence communing with him or having just seen him use you to reveal himself to someone else, you know what I'm talking about. At such moments it seems time itself stands still. Waves of joy sweep across us and it is so incredible, that you feel if you were made just for that one moment your life would have had a wealth of meaning. "I was made for this."

And you were.

Jesus knew that about himself. Faced with two choices, "Father, save me!" or "Father, glorify your name," he chose the latter. He knew the only real glory existed in fulfilling the Father's purpose in his life regardless of the circumstances. As much as he might have dreaded the agony of the cross, he knew he had come into the world for that moment.

"Father glorify your name."

This is the prayer that the Father always answers. "Father, may the purpose for which you have created me and placed me where you have in the world be fulfilled completely." It is the prayer that disarms our self-interest and asserts our trust that the Father who made us and who loves us so deeply knows us better than we know ourselves.

We make this choice not one time for our entire life; but in the immediacy of each situation we face. When I didn't get the job I wanted, the raise I deserved, or the medical report I hoped for: "Father, save me!" or "Father, glorify your name."

We face it when we're the subject of malicious gossip or the object of someone's selfish act. "Father, save me!" or "Father, glorify your name."

We confront it when we face people in need, the opportunity to speak the truth where it will cost us, or when we can take up the cause of the powerless. "Father, save me!" or "Father, glorify your name."

We engage it when the dark storm surrounds us, and when trials overwhelm us. "Father, save me!" or "Father, glorify your name."

A DAILY CHOICE

It's not the words we use that matter here, but the cry of our heart. Choose to save yourself and you will find yourself resisting God when you don't even mean to. You'll end up praying against the very things God is using to transform you. You'll miss his attempts to help because they won't look like the thing you want.

I've got to be honest. I have spent most of my life praying "save me" prayers. I didn't always know that's what I was doing, but simply thinking that God would want the best for me defined in my terms.

But God has taught me over and over again in this journey that he knows best about everything. The way I would solve my problems and help other people would do more damage to us all than he would allow. When he denied me the thing that I wanted it was because he had a better way not only to deal with my circumstance but change me in the process. In almost every situation it seems that what God is doing is the opposite of what I would do.

When he wanted to teach me to trust him more, I prayed he would fix things so I wouldn't have to.

When he wanted to lead me into the fullest participation of what he made me to be, I prayed he would just make me happy.

When he wanted to change my character so I would represent his heart to others, I wanted him to leave me the way I was and not allow me to be caught in situations where the "old Wayne" would surface.

I'm so glad he won, more often in spite of my prayers than because of them. I want him to continue, I really do. I want him to use everything in my life to shape me to be more like him so that he can fulfill in me the purpose for which he made me.

FINAL WORDS

I could go on with other implications of what it means to live in God's love, but I think you the picture is clear enough now and you'll be able to recognize the pathway and follow it wherever your Father wants to take you. This is a life far better lived than it is read about.

Besides, this life is far more fun to discover than it is to let someone tell you about it. As you find yourself falling into the security of the Father's love you will find that your own thoughts, ideas and actions will surprise you.

You'll catch yourself thinking, "I'm not like this." And yet you are. You always have been, it's just that it was distorted and twisted by a broken relationship with the Father who love most. Find some others who are sharing the same journey and you'll have the joy of discovering what they are learning as well.

The journey cannot be found in the pages of this book or any other. It lies in the Father's heart and your own.

I can't make this happen for you, so I won't even try.

You can't make it happen for you, so please don't you try either.

What you can do is trust God enough to let him do it for you. Don't worry about having any illusions there. He seems to love doing this more than anything else he does and he's been doing it with people through the whole course of history.

If you came into a room where a two-year-old child was playing and wanted to have a relationship with that child, who would have to make that happen? Would it be the child? Of course not. To forge a relationship with that toddler, you must be the one to do it. He'll have to respond of course; but you would take the initiative. You would find a way to meet him at his level and you would engage him with things that interest him as you draw him into a relationship.

The same is true with God. He is higher above you than you are above a two-year-old. He will take the initiative at your invitation. Simply ask him to begin to reveal to you how much he loves you and he will ably take it from there.

"Glorify your name."

In all of us, now until the end of the age.
And for eternity beyond.
Amen.

> *In him we were also chosen... according to the plan of him
> who works out everything in conformity with the pur-
> pose of his will, in order that we... might be for the praise
> of his glory.*
>
> —EPHESIANS 1:11-12

For your personal journey

Review the things you are currently praying about these days.
Which prayers are "save me" prayers and which are "glorify
your name" prayers? Which serve your desires and which result
from your understanding of God's purpose in the situations
you're in? Ask him to reveal to you every day what his purpose is
in the circumstances you face and pray for its continued
unfolding as he draws you closer to himself.

Discussion Questions

Chapter 1 &. Daisy Petal Christianity

1. Share an experience you went through in which you really doubted if God cared about you.
2. How do you feel about it now? If you're still unsure, what might you ask God to do to change your perception of that event.
3. If you look back now and know that God loved you even if you didn't recognize it at the time, what did you learn in the process?
4. How can we encourage one another to be certain of God's love instead of doubtful?

Chapter 2 &. What the Disciples Didn't Know

1. Share your favorite Bible story of God revealing himself to someone.
2. What do you see in the relationship Jesus had with his disciples that you want to see in your own relationship with him?
3. Share an experience from your own life when you knew God's presence was with you in some tangible way.
4. Spend a few moments talking about what we can do to grow to know God better.

He Loves Me!

Chapter 3 ಿ Threatened With Hell

1. Why do religious people use the threat of hell to get people to come to God?
2. When you think of God appearing in your life, what do you see? How would he act, and what does he feel about you? Would you see Jesus treating you the same way if he showed up? How do we reconcile the two?
3. Think about the relationship that Jesus has offered us with his Father. What might we say about that to communicate to people who don't know him just what kind of God he is?
4. Ask God to free you from fearing his judgment and teach you instead how to trust his love.

Chapter 4 ಿ A Father Like No Other

1. Take a moment to share whether or not you identify more with the older son or the younger son and why.
3. What did you learn about God's love in this parable?
3. What kinds of things have you done when you've felt "less-loved" by God?
4. Think of some ways that God has demonstrated his love for you, even when you did nothing to earn it.

Chapter 5 ಿ Welcome Home

1. Have you ever felt like that stray puppy, afraid to trust because of past disappointments.
2. Recall some of the events from Abraham's story (Genesis 12-23) that God used to teach him trust.
3. Share your own stories of how God has taught you to trust him in the past.
4. What are some of the ways we can grow to know God's love better?

Chapter 6 ಿ The Tyranny of the Favor Line

1. Have you ever felt like the woman with the sick child? How did you resolve those moments in your life?
2. Where do you feel like you walk the tightrope of the favor line in your relationship with God? Where do you feel guilt for not doing enough?
3. Read Saul's conversion from Acts 9:1-9. Why did Jesus do this for him? What do you think Saul did to qualify for this moment?
4. Pray together that God will teach you how to know him as he really is.

Chapter 7 ❧ What Shall I Give to God?

1. What kinds of gifts and offerings do people use today to try to earn God's affection?
2. Have you ever gone through a season like Janice did, working harder, but feeling emptier spiritually? What can you learn from that experience?
3. Was there a time in your life when you sensed that Father was delighted with you? Was that because you had done something big for him, or you just knew that he loved you just the way you were?
4. Pray together that God will teach you how to find your acceptance in his love alone and not in anything you can do for him, or give to him.

Chapter 8 ❧ The Businessman and the Beggar

1. Are you more like the businessman or the beggar in this chapter? Explain why.
2. Describe the bars you've tried to jump over to merit God's favor.
3. Why do you think that we have been given so many bars to jump over as proof that we are serious about God's life?
4. What would it be like if you could trust God's mercy for you every day?
5. Pray for each other that you'll learn the difference between mercy and performance.

Chapter 9 ❧ The God We Love to Fear

1. Of the list of fears presented in this chapter, which ones do we normally think are helpful to us? Which ones are harmful? Which ones do you battle the most in your daily life?
2. Has your fear of the Lord helped you avoid harmful actions in your life?
3. Has it been enough to make you stop sinning completely?
4. Tell about a time when the fear of the Lord was very real to you. How did that fear affect your relationship with him?
5. Respond together to what you've shared in prayer, asking God to free you from the slavery of fear.

Chapter 10 ❧ The Most Powerful Force in the Universe

1. Today if Jesus asked you the same question he asked Peter, how would you respond?
2. What things do you do for God that seem motivated by your fear of him or his judgments against you?
3. What things do you do that seem to flow out of knowing that God loves you?
4. Compare those experiences motivated by fear and those by love. How do you feel in each circumstance?
5. Read I John 4:7-21 and identify the specific things John identifies about God's love.
6. Pray together that God will increasingly reveal the depth of his love for each of you.

Chapter 11 ❧ He Loved You Enough to Let You Go

1. Explain and discuss the following: One can obey without trusting; but one cannot trust without obeying.
2. Think of some moments in your life when your efforts to do good only backfired and made the situation worse.
3. What kinds of things does the enemy whisper in your ear to drive a wedge between you and God so that your trust in him is eroded?
4. What do you think God can do to help you trust him more?

Chapter 12 ❧ Who Needed the Sacrifice?

1. Reflect together on the truth that the True God is the one who wants to sacrifice for us instead of one demanding our sacrifices for him.
2. Where do you still try to appease God in the sacrifices you make, or in blaming others to alleviate your guilt?
3. How does this change the way you view Christianity?
4. Spend some moments thanking God together for providing all that we need to come into a trusting relationship with him.

Chapter 13 ❧ The Hen and Her Chicks

1. What did you get out of the story of the hen and her chicks?
2. Have you ever used religion as a covering for shame? How?
3. What is easier for you to do, run under his wing or try to figure out a way to fix things yourself? Why do you think that is?
4. Give examples of God's unlimited patience and celebrate together in prayer his awesome faithfulness to the weakest of his people.

Chapter 14 ✑ What Really Happened on the Cross?

1. Together share how the story of the cross has touched your life. What events stick out in your mind?
2. What do you see going on between the Father and the Son through those moments?
3. What does it mean to you that Jesus became sin itself? Share your ideas together.
4. Read one of the crucifixion accounts and give thanks together for the indescribable lengths God would go to so that we might have life in his name.

Chapter 15 ✑ The Antidote for Sin

1. Can you think of a time when your love for someone caused you to act on their behalf at great personal risk?
2. How does seeing God's wrath as the antidote for sin, rather than its punishment affect your view of God and the cross?
3. Talk about the difference between the cup he drank and the cup he offers us to drink. How does that touch you?
4. Ask God together to give each of you a personal revelation of the cross and confidence in all God accomplished there for you.

Chapter 16 ✑ In the Darkest Moment...Trust

1. How would your life be different if you absolutely, completely trusted God for every thing in your life?
2. Where does the darkness seem to surround you and make it difficult to understand what God is doing in you?
3. How can Jesus' actions on the cross provide the basis for you to learn how to trust Jesus through anything life can hurl at you?
4. Pray for each other that God would teach you in the every day realities of your life what it is to trust that he is with you, working out his will in you.

HE LOVES ME!

Chapter 17 ✑ Trying to Earn Points With Someone Who Is No Longer Keeping Score

1. What kinds of things do we count to determine our status with God?
2. When you feel as if you're not doing enough for God, what do you usually focus on?
3. Have you tried to do some great thing for God? How did it turn out? Did he use it to touch some lives anyway? (Isn't he amazing?)
4. What would you do tomorrow if you absolutely knew God loved you and just wanted to share your life?
5. What barrier(s) do you see in your life that makes it difficult for you to accept God's love for you? Pray together that God will show you how to get past them.

Chapter 18 ✑ A Lifetime of Learning to Trust

1. Talk about grace as you understood it in the past in contrast to what you read in this chapter.
2. What add-ons to grace have you tried? Did they work?
3. How do you find yourself viewing sin, as a forbidden pleasure or a destroying presence?
4. Share and incident where you experienced righteousness that grew naturally out of simply learning to trust God instead of leaning on yourself?
5. Where do you see yourself putting the demands of righteousness before the joys of relationship? Pray that God will help you reverse this process and learn to delight in him.

Chapter 19 ✑ So Sin Isn't Important to God?

1. Share some experiences of how the Father has taught you to trust him when you've been at the end of your rope.
2. Read Romans 8:31-32 and discuss how the cross guarantees that the Father loves you today in the midst of whatever circumstances you are facing.
3. Even though the advice, "You just need to trust God more," is true, why is it the worst possible advice to give someone in the midst of a crisis?
4. Explore why we only seem to be able to support someone when we understand what they are going through. How can we support people on their journey even though God is doing things in their life that neither they nor we may understand?
5. Ask God together to teach you how to walk out this trust in the everyday circumstances of your life.

DISCUSSION QUESTIONS

Chapter 20 ✑ Shamelessly Free

1. Share some of the ways you see shame working in your life.
2. How do you cover up for it?
3. How would your life and fellowship together be different if you cared what the Father thought of you more than anyone else?
4. We have all heard the tapes of shame playing in our heads. Take a few moments to identify some of the things God wants you to know about the way he thinks of you.

Chapter 21 ✑ In Exactly the Same Way

1. Share together some of the best moments in your life when God expressed his love to you through another believer. What made it special to you?
2. Talk about some of the things that make relationships helpful and what makes them harmful.
3. Where should our focus be if we don't find ourselves compassionately involved with people around us?
4. If you're a group that meets regularly together, ask God over the next couple of weeks if there is a specific way your group might express God's love together to someone. Don't think of a program to start here, unless he tells you clearly to do that; but rather think in terms of something practical you can do to bless someone without manipulating them.

Chapter 22 ✑ The Prayer God Always Answers

1. Give examples from Scripture and from your own life of "save me" prayers?
2. Now give examples of "Father, glorify your name" prayers.
3. Can you think of a time in your life when you prayed for the exact opposite of what you wanted because you felt God's purpose would be fulfilled by it? Share about that.
4. If some in your group are open to share some of the things they're praying about, ask God to show you together what his purpose is and how it will best be served by your prayers.
5. Pray for God to be glorified in each of your lives as the journey unfolds in the days ahead.

Wayne Jacobsen directs Lifestream Ministries and travels the world teaching on themes of intimacy with God and relational church life. He is a Contributing Editor to *Leadership Journal* and the author of *The Naked Church*, *In My Father's Vineyard* and *Tales of the Vine*. Wayne also works as a trainer and mediator in public education, helping build bridges of cooperation and understanding where the issues of church and state collide. He resides with his wife, Sara, in Oxnard, California.

For further information about Wayne's writings or to invite him to share with your group, please contact him at:

Lifestream Ministries
P.O. Box 50240
Oxnard, CA 93031
805.988.4409
http://www.lifestream.org
waynej@lifestream.org

Other Books by Wayne Jacobsen

The Naked Church
The Vineyard
Tales of the Vine
Pathways of Grace
In My Father's Vineyard